Editor-in-Chief and Founder:
  *Lyndon H. LaRouche, Jr.*
Editorial Board: *Lyndon H. LaRouche, Jr. , Helga
  Zepp-LaRouche, Paul Gallagher, Tony Papert,
  Gerald Rose, Dennis Small, Jeffrey Steinberg,
  William Wertz*
Co-Editors: *Paul Gallagher, Tony Papert*
Managing Editor: *Nancy Spannaus*
Technology: *Marsha Freeman*
Books: *Katherine Notley*
Ebooks: *Richard Burden*
Graphics: *Alan Yue*
Photos: *Stuart Lewis*
Circulation Manager: *Stanley Ezrol*

INTELLIGENCE DIRECTORS
Counterintelligence: *Jeffrey Steinberg, Michele
  Steinberg*
Economics: *John Hoefle, Marcia Merry Baker,
  Paul Gallagher*
History: *Anton Chaitkin*
Ibero-America: *Dennis Small*
Russia and Eastern Europe: *Rachel Douglas*
United States: *Debra Freeman*

INTERNATIONAL BUREAUS
Bogotá: *Miriam Redondo*
Berlin: *Rainer Apel*
Copenhagen: *Tom Gillesberg*
Houston: *Harley Schlanger*
Lima: *Sara Madueño*
Melbourne: *Robert Barwick*
Mexico City: *Gerardo Castilleja Chávez*
New Delhi: *Ramtanu Maitra*
Paris: *Christine Bierre*
Stockholm: *Ulf Sandmark*
United Nations, N.Y.C.: *Leni Rubinstein*
Washington, D.C.: *William Jones*
Wiesbaden: *Göran Haglund*

ON THE WEB
e-mail: eirns@larouchepub.com
www.larouchepub.com
www.executiveintelligencereview.com
www.larouchepub.com/eiw
Webmaster: *John Sigerson*
Assistant Webmaster: *George Hollis*
Editor, Arabic-language edition: *Hussein Askary*

EIR (ISSN 0273-6314) *is published weekly
(50 issues), by EIR News Service, Inc.,
P.O. Box 17390, Washington, D.C. 20041-0390.
(703) 777-9451*

**European Headquarters:** E.I.R. GmbH, Postfach
Bahnstrasse 9a, D-65205, Wiesbaden, Germany
Tel: 49-611-73650
Homepage: http://www.eirna.com
e-mail: eirna@eirna.com
Director: Georg Neudecker

**Montreal, Canada:** 514-461-1557

**Denmark:** EIR - Danmark, Sankt Knuds Vej 11,
basement left, DK-1903 Frederiksberg, Denmark.
Tel.: +45 35 43 60 40, Fax: +45 35 43 87 57. e-mail:
eirdk@hotmail.com.

**Mexico City:** EIR, Sor Juana Inés de la Cruz 242-2
Col. Agricultura C.P. 11360
Delegación M. Hidalgo, México D.F.
Tel. (5525) 5318-2301
eirmexico@gmail.com

Canada Post Publication Sales Agreement
#40683579

**Postmaster:** Send all address changes to *EIR*, P.O.
Box 17390, Washington, D.C. 20041-0390.

Signed articles in *EIR* represent the views of the
authors, and not necessarily those of the Editorial
Board.

# Foreclose on Wall St. Save the Nation

# EIR Contents

www.larouchepub.com   Volume 42, Number 34, August 28, 2015

## Cover This Week

*A view of Wall Street*

# The Biggest Financial Crisis In Modern History

*Lyndon H. LaRouche, Jr. addressed the LaRouche PAC Policy Committee in the following terms on Monday, August 24.*

What happened this weekend was the biggest international financial crisis in modern history. The dimensions which I've indicated by those remarks will become clearer very rapidly during the course of the day, and the following day. My concern here is to identify what the problem is in the first case, and secondly what the solution to the problem may be in the second case.

What happened essentially was—we were aware of this. I was acutely aware of this during this past Saturday, and knew that this great crisis, this collapse, which is a trans-Atlantic collapse primarily, was coming on. And so we had our meetings, which were at various locations inside the United States; and we discussed these things, and we assigned Jeff Steinberg to take responsibility for reporting the facts which I had presented. And that was done.

Now what happened, of course, is after the weekend, today, on Monday, the fact that this collapse *had occurred*, became manifest. This is not unusual. When something is breaking down on Sunday, and the newspapers aren't functioning to deal with that problem, then they have to do it on Monday. And that's what happened.

But this is the biggest crash in the trans-Atlantic community *in all modern history*. This is what's happened. And therefore, what we have to define is: what is the nature of the crisis; and what is the solution for the crisis? In other words, you just can't interpret things, because we already knew it was happening. In our discussions on Friday and Saturday, it was apparent to me that this was about to happen. So we made that the subject of our telephonic discussion—and it's now there. But it is actually the *greatest financial crisis in modern history*.

Now on first looking at it, you say: "Well, is this like the Wall Street collapse—1933 and so forth?" Well, somewhat, but that was a little one. This is the big one. And the problem is, we have to state what the case is; I have to state the case in particular, in order to get the right solution. The danger now is the wrong solution, which is what most people will tend to do.

They try to say:

- "Well, this will solve the problem."
- "Well, we have to do this in order to avoid the problem."
- "We have to do this for that reason."
- "Well, maybe there's hope."

Another one of those things that goes past. There is no hope, not in the ordinary sense.

What's happened is that what we call Wall Street in the United States, in particular, is the model case of the collapse *which has just occurred*. Now that means that the Wall Street institutions are about to be cancelled, blown out, because they have no basis to sustain them. In other words, they don't do anything. Wall Street does not *do* anything in its practice, which is beneficial to human beings. It only benefits non-human beings, like Wall Street creatures. And they are about to get washed out.

## Much, Much Bigger Than FDR's Crisis

Now therefore, what we have to do primarily, is pull together an international discussion in which we don't just do an emergency. This is something much bigger than what Franklin Roosevelt dealt with, when he went into the Presidency. This is much, much bigger. Because the degree of destruction, the relative degree of destruction to the American population, to the American system, is far, far greater than anything that we have ever known in U.S. experience before.

So essentially, what we have to do, is we have to take Wall Street itself—that is, that system, the Wall Street system—and *fold it*, shut it down. And we have to introduce new programs which provide a credit system for getting people back to work, getting people who haven't had jobs, work; people who don't have medical care, treatment, who need these things. This must happen. And we must simply accept,—and don't weep, don't weep over the disasters that they are suffering, that the Wall Street crowd is now expressing, howling about. They have *nothing* coming to them but pain, essentially.

And therefore, what we have to do quickly, is change the laws. Now one model for this, a good approximation for what we have to do in the United States, in particular, but also for the trans-Atlantic community, in general: what we have to do, is immediately create a system of investments which will actually have the effect of providing actual physical progress in the condition of life of the citizens of the United States, and comparable treatment for people in Europe. This is where the immediate crisis is located.

China has absorbed a crisis, which is a by-product of this thing that hit Wall Street and London. But that's not as crucial. China is in a better situation. Russia is in a better situation than any other part of Europe. Now Russia has got a tough situation, and we understand that. But Russia is in a better situation *morally*, and economically, than Europe in general, and certainly the United States in general.

Well, the United States has a lot of power, in terms of thermonuclear power, but that isn't going to do you much good; to get thermonuclear power thrust down your throat is not a good medicine.

So therefore, what we have to do, is we have to shut down Wall Street,—*shut it down!* A mercy killing, if you please. Shut it down. Then we have to go to a President Roosevelt turn, but on a much larger scale than Franklin Roosevelt had to do it. What we have to do is actually organize productive employment. Now the problem is, in the United States we have very few people who are qualified for *productive* employment. We have a lot of people who are half-slave and half-man, children who are almost not human, under the influence of these present kinds of conditions. These things have to be corrected.

But the main thing we have to do, for the United States in particular, is to restore confidence in the American people by giving them reason to believe that they can have confidence. And that means that we're going to have to do on a grand scale, what was the same intention that Franklin Roosevelt had in his time,—but this is a much bigger one. It's global.

And this is the danger of war, thermonuclear war, coming from Obama, for example. Obama has put the United States itself on the edge of thermonuclear war, which means that most of the people in the United States are going to be extinguished, burned up, quick, in one blow-up.

So therefore, what we have to do is re-organize the economy on the basis of the principles of what our great President had done. And that's the chance. Without that, there is no real solution. But there's no way you can compromise. There is no way you can not write off these funds, which are now bankrupt funds; you have to eliminate them, cancel them. And you have to immediately act to launch programs which will replace these kinds of things, replace them by actual productive development. It's possible and we have to do it.

It's necessary specifically in the United States, in the trans-Atlantic community, especially in the Northern parts of the trans-Atlantic community, and so forth. That means the biggest operation mankind has ever undertaken; because we have to move quickly. Especially in the trans-Atlantic community, we have to move quickly to prevent a catastrophe.

And that's where we are. Now I have a lot more to say on this, but I think my having said this much opens up the discussion for a broader examination of what's at stake here.

# Wall Street is Totally Bankrupt

*Excerpts from Thursday, August 20, 2015 LaRouche PAC Activists' 'Fireside Chat' with Lyndon LaRouche.*

**John Ascher:** Good evening, everyone. This is John Ascher welcoming you to the 14th Fireside Chat with Lyndon LaRouche. Lyn, I'm hoping you are on the phone and can hear me.

**Lyndon LaRouche**: I can hear you and I'm on the phone.

**Ascher:** Are there any preliminary remarks that you would like to make?

**LaRouche**: Just simply, broadly, that we've had successes in terms of Manhattan and the Manhattan developments, which really are complementing exactly what we're doing here, on this occasion as part of an integral process.

Obviously, this thing is not going to remain in the same form. It's going to evolve into a more systematic form, a higher form, of discussions as actually making decisions on the future of the nation. So I think what we're doing now is a preliminary process, of getting a larger organization, more coherently brought together,

but that means that people have to become more familiar with each other. And this is a process we have to go through in order to develop a more coherent approach to the whole national challenge, and international challenge, which we face right now.

**Q:** Good evening, John, and good evening, Lyn. This is B— from New Jersey. This is going to be more in the form of a report. And as a number of people, particularly in the Manhattan Project area, know, I had had published down in Florida, a letter to the editor, basically saying that Hillary Clinton can do the nation and the world a big favor by coming clean on Benghazi, and paving the way for eliminating Obama from the Presidency, such that we can effect the necessary change to head off the drive for thermonuclear war.

Now, I had also sent in to the local papers here in New Jersey, that same letter, which had not been published in the local papers. But what I did was, I took a copy of the letter to the editor published in Florida, and I resubmitted it to the local newspapers, saying "I wish you'd reconsider not publishing my letter, and use what

Schiller Institute

*Success in Manhattan: The Schiller Institute chorus at the August 15, 2015 Musical Evening.*

they did in Florida in the newspaper, to give you a little impetus to publish it."

### You Have to Get Obama Out Now

I know there's also an event which I went to yesterday, up in Manhattan at Dante Park. And on the way up there, I took a copy of that letter also, and a copy of the petition that Helga had written and that we have

---

**The point is, you have to get Obama out of the Presidency now, or you're not going to have a United States of living people in it. And that's really the short thing, and that's the real story.**

---

been circulating, and took that to a Congressional office on my way up to Manhattan; along with some other material requesting a meeting with the Congressman.

So, this morning I get up and one of the papers I had resubmitted my letter-to-the-editor to, published the "Clinton Must Come Clean on Benghazi," and actually put it right alongside of a letter to the editor by one of the local Congressmen, whose office had refused to meet with me on a number of things; and in fact, when I did talk to him on the phone, had said, "impeaching Obama's not going to happen." So obviously, something's going on there, that they would publish my letter to the editor, right next to his letter to the editor.

But then, a couple of hours later, I got a call from another Congressional office, the one that I had dropped material off to yesterday, and they had requested a meeting for this coming week, on whatever matters I wanted to bring to the Congressman's attention.

So I just wanted to bring that up; I know somebody's going to give a report later on the event yesterday in Dante Park in Manhattan. But I did want to make clear to people that perseverance can overcome.

**LaRouche:** Well, the point is, on this whole issue, that there is a fraud; Hillary committed a fraud, but under pressure from Obama. And Obama lied! And in the entire matter from that point on, Hillary backed down, cheapened herself, and has not recovered her honor since that time.

I mean, she tried to tell the truth, that Obama has lied in the matter of Benghazi; but she backed down from it when he put pressure on her. But what he had

said was a *lie*. So Obama is a consistent *liar*; that's his most common characteristic.

But he's also a real thug. He takes after his step father, who was a thug. And putting this guy in the Presidency, was done by the British Monarchy, and that system put Obama into place. Now, we had a Bush family there before then, and they weren't much good at all; but Obama is worse than any and all Bushes combined, himself!

### Cancel Wall Street

And the issue here is, Hillary has not come forth to reaffirm what *she said and knew*. And by her playing a game of not challenging Obama, when she *had* the facts to challenge him, she corrupted herself, and she's going through spinning, and spinning, and spinning. She's destroying herself in every respect by submitting to a lie that she knows was a lie, because she identified it! And that's what the issue is.

The point is, *you have to get Obama out of the Presidency now, or you're not going to have a United States of living people in it.* And that's really the short thing, and that's the real story. The thing became more complicated, more complicated; explanations, explanations, explanations around it, but none of it's true! Obama lied! Period! And he intimidated Hillary into lying, too. And she's suffering the fact that she submitted to the lies imposed upon her by Obama. And Obama is the criminal. And we will not have a Presidency much longer, unless we get Obama thrown out of it.

**Q:** Lyndon, this is J— from Fredericksburg, Virginia. My question is, John Kerry recently made a statement about the reserve currency of the United States; I don't know if you recall that or not, but do you actually agree with this statement: If we did not find that Iran deal, that the United States would no longer be the reserve currency?

**LaRouche:** Well, that's a complicated way to put it. It's really rather simple. Look, what we have is, Franklin Roosevelt provided a standard for our currency under his Administration. Now, what happened then, is that was cancelled. And what came in was this business of speculation, Wall Street speculation particularly. That destroyed us.

Now, if we're going to get a U.S. currency which is functional, we simply have to shut down Wall Street, because Wall Street's mechanism is the thing that has

Since that time, there's been a continuing drift further and further away from that policy. As a result, terrible things have happened to the welfare of most of our people. And we need to get back to that. We can solve the problem: All we have to do, is get rid of some of these

---

**We have to get rid of the Obama Administration. We have to return to a Glass-Steagall policy, and which we call the Glass-Steagall system, which is the name given to it by Franklin Roosevelt.**

**Now, what that would mean, is we would strip out a lot of claims against American citizens in the U.S. economy. And we would immediately create a credit system, which would actually encourage investment in productive endeavors. It would mean an improvement in terms of the economy on the economic side, on the educational side; it would mean we would go to a much higher rate of productivity per capita; it would mean a recovery from most of the things that we suffer from in recent times here.**

---

laws that were stuck in there, contrary to Franklin Roosevelt's plan.

### We Can Launch Recovery Now

Franklin Roosevelt saved the United States during his service: After that, there was disruption, erosion, corrosion; some successes, and some failures; more failures than successes. We could, if we understood the history of our nation, the United States, we could easily pick out, at least from experts as such, pick out the exact measures needed to start a general recovery program for the United States. And it would not be just a recovery program in the economic sense, but in a sense of development of the powers of mind of the human personality.

We have been destroyed, to a large degree, by the things that have been imposed upon the American people, and we simply have to do those things that

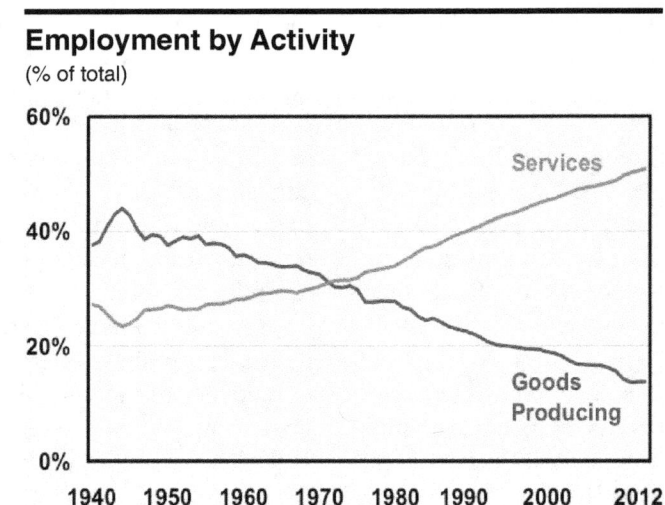

**Employment by Activity**
(% of total)

*This graph of the decline of goods-producing jobs in the United States, shows that the process began almost immediately after the death of FDR, and accelerated after the demise of Glass-Steagall in 1999.*

Franklin Roosevelt had pioneered in doing, and do it all over again. And that will be a tough road to go, but it will be a road to success.

**Q:** [via internet] Lyn I have a question from YouTube from T—, who, I believe, may be from Texas. And he says that you've previously pointed out that we have to define the next step in, as he puts it, "human self-evolution." He asks you, Lyn: "How would you define a mission for humanity from a Galactic perspective?"

**LaRouche:** Well, the Galactic perspective is a very good place to start from. Because the Galaxy is—well, probably I should explain something, so as not to confuse anybody.

We've had different ideas of how mankind could progress. We had, at a certain point, under Kepler,—Kepler defined the Solar System itself. And that worked, but it was not adequate. But the fact is that what his discovery was, was absolutely essential for the progress of mankind. But, it wasn't the complete progress of mankind.

So, therefore, we now realize there was a higher level of standard for measure of the progress of mankind. We now recognize that as being the Galactic Principle; that is, the Galaxy has a superior force in the universe, with respect to mankind and other kinds of things, and is a standard which we now use as a measure of the methods we must apply to the continuation of the existence of mankind in the Solar System, and so forth.

### Mankind's Progress

And, what's involved here, is that mankind is the only creature that can make true scientific discoveries,—that is, discoveries of scientific principle. And these, generally, are in accord with the legacy of the Galaxy, also Kepler's own work. And this progress of each generation to rise a little bit higher, in terms of understanding of, and mastery of, the universe that we're living in, is the name of progress. And that's called scientific progress, true scientific progress.

True scientific progress, physical scientific progress, is actually the difference of mankind from mere animals. Animals have certain abilities, but they're fixed by species. Mankind, unlike the animals, mankind has the ability to rise to a higher level, successively; to make discoveries, which mankind has never been able to understand before, and to use those discoveries to bring mankind into a state of power within the Solar System, within the universe, to make discoveries by which mankind will advance greatly into higher levels of operation. Like the discovery, for example, of Kepler—the discovery of the Solar System by Kepler; that was the great step. You have the discovery of the Galactic System now, another great step.

And by understanding these great steps in knowledge, and the practice of knowledge, mankind is able to have seemingly limitless opportunities for its future. And that's really, I think, the most inspiring thing what we can think of.

Q: [via internet] Well, inspired by that idea, I have a question from M—, who says, "I'd like you to say something about the connection between the national policies that you are advocating and the nation's educational policy. What should we be teaching our youth, and how? I have been using your 1986 essay, 'Saving Our Children: Reintroducing Classical Education to the Secondary Classroom,' as a grounding for my course work towards an education degree."

So she wants to know if you could say something about how these things would apply in terms of bringing them into the education system?

**The Educational Process**

LaRouche: Well, the first thing is you have to look to a fundamental principle here, that is, that mankind's progress is expressed in mankind's discovery of a principle of action: that is, a practical principle of action which will enable mankind as a species, to make a step up to a higher level of achievement within the Solar System or whatever. That's the issue. And the education

system is to promote the education of students, young people, students, etc., and to bring each of them into a higher understanding of something that mankind had never known before. In this experience of discovering a truth which was never known before, is the distinction of the human species from everything else.

The educational process, or what we should consider the educational process, corresponds to that. Einstein, for example, in the Twentieth Century, Einstein

> And this progress of each generation to rise a little bit higher, in terms of understanding of, and mastery of, the universe that we're living in, is the name of progress. And that's called scientific progress, true scientific progress.

was the paragon of a mind which understood the future in a conception, where all the other scientists of that period, or that century, were a little bit, not too smart, Einstein was uniquely superior. Why? Because he was looking into the actual creation of the future.

And that's the distinction of mankind, of human beings from animals: that mankind progresses through the human mind into higher levels of existence than had been known before. That is, to know principles, to discover principles of action which mankind had never known before. And the purpose of mankind is to discover the experience of those things, those effects, and that is what human progress is. And that's the distinction of the human being from a mere animal.

Ascher: [Question indistinct] So, Lyn, he's really asking the difference between positive law and natural law and what is the basis upon which we're fighting?

LaRouche: Well, the point of law is the principle of progress. In other words, the intention of mankind is in life,—mankind as a process also, not just as an individual but as a process... The problem is that mankind must rise to higher levels of achievement in terms of effect. You know, progress, economic progress, cultural progress, all these kinds of things which are well-known to us as phenomena. That's what the intention is.

**On to Still-Higher Levels**

Because the point is that mankind is a unique species, when properly understood. Mankind is always going higher, to a higher level of achievement, in science, in technology, in every other way; and that's the standard, and that's what the difference is of mankind from animals. Animals are not capable of rising to higher levels of development of practice. Only human beings can do that.

The object in life, therefore, is for mankind to progress, to rise to higher standards of achievement; and scientific principles, for example, the practice of scientific principles, is one of the most characteristic features of progress. And the way in which, through the educational process, through higher experimentation and so forth, these are means by which mankind becomes mankind, as opposed to merely animals.

Mankind is not an animal. Mankind is defined as a creature which rises, always, to a *higher level of existence*, whereas no animal can do that. And that's what the standard is.

EIRNS/Stuart Lewis

*Upgrading education: A youth studying geometric construction at a Schiller Institute daycamp in 2004.*

**Ascher:** Lyn, I think that's a good point where we can conclude here this evening. I just want to mention one thing to people on the phone, which I'll send out in

my email tomorrow following up from our call this evening: the video of the musical performance that was mentioned before, the Music Evening, the *Musikabend* that was so beautiful and held last Saturday night in Manhattan. So I would encourage people to make sure you look at that, because we want to radiate this process from New York throughout the country.

Lyn, is there anything you would like to say in concluding remarks?

**LaRouche:** Yes. The point is, in New York right now, we had an achievement—we must call it an achievement—in bringing together a chorus, a choral phenomenon which was quite successful. The fact of that success is not merely something where you get pats on the back or something, but is an effect in which the people participating, feel themselves as being uplifted by the process which they have shared in going through. And that thing that happened in that New York meeting, was *excellent*, and the spirit was excellent; the improvement in satisfaction among the participants, was *excellent*. And we must expect to go to still higher levels in the coming weeks.

**Ascher:** Lyn, thank you very much. This has been our 14th discussion here. And we look forward with being back you next Thursday. That concludes our 14th Fireside Chat with Lyndon LaRouche. Good night, Lyn.

**LaRouche:** Good night.

destroyed the integrity of the U.S. economy, and put it into an actual chaotic situation that has ruined the people of the United States. So therefore, you have to go back to a Glass-Steagall policy, which Hillary will not accept—so she's a menace, too! We've got to get back to a Glass-Steagall standard.

## Back to Glass-Steagall

Now, what would that mean? This requires a little explanation; what's that mean? That means that the Wall Street money is worthless; it's absolutely worthless. It's phony money. And what would happen is, if we did the thing properly, we would essentially cancel Wall Street; we'd cancel all those games. Because that's what caused the problem! From a process from Franklin Roosevelt, who has actually solved the problem; then you had various steps to undermine what Franklin Roosevelt had accomplished, which was the Glass-Steagall principle as such.

If we go back to Glass-Steagall, that means we wipe out all of those kinds of debts, Wall Street debts,—just cancel them! They're worthless, they are presently worthless. They are worth nothing, or less than nothing. And Wall Street is totally bankrupt; the British system has a similar kind of problem, the total bankruptcy of the whole system in its present form.

A reform, in the case of the United States, or in the current case of the British system right now, if you go back to a Glass-Steagall-type of approach, the Franklin Roosevelt type, you would immediately cancel *most of the debt* which is claimed to be the property of the British system, and of the current U.S. system. Now you just wipe that out, because Wall Street is hopelessly bankrupt; it's worth less than nothing. That's the problem.

All we have to do, is go back to a Glass-Steagall standard: The minute we do that, we can now start the march toward an economic recovery of the United States system. That's the simple story.

**Q:** Hi, this is A— in Minnesota. I'm curious about the Iran issue. And it seems to me as if Obama is contradicting his past behavior on most all international agreements, relations; it seems as if he's always on the side of chaos and destruction. Well, what exactly is happening with this Iran negotiation? And I know Congress has to OK it; and it seems as if Obama is—he's on the right side, for what reason I don't know!

## Create a Credit System

**LaRouche:** Obama's on the wrong side, always. It's the only side he has. [laughs] No, the man really should never have been President. There is big doubt to be placed on how the British system created the Obama administration. That was a British operation.

And what he's done, on the record, what Obama has done in his candidacy and in the results of his candi-

---

If we go back to Glass-Steagall, that means we wipe out all of those kinds of debts, Wall Street debts,—just cancel them! They're worthless, they are presently worthless. They are worth nothing, or less than nothing. And Wall Street is totally bankrupt.

---

dacy, is largely fraud, wild-eyed fraud. What it's done to the conditions of the American people is monstrous. Therefore, this guy should be removed from office, and we should investigate whether he's committed crimes or not. The penalties under law for the crimes he's committed are massive and extensive. The lies are abundant; the whole thing is a fraud.

We have to get rid of the Obama administration. We have to return to a Glass-Steagall policy, and which we call the Glass-Steagall system, which is the name given to it by Franklin Roosevelt; go back in that direction.

Now, what that would mean, is we would strip out a lot of claims against American citizens in the U.S. economy. And we would immediately create a credit system, which would actually encourage investment in productive endeavors. It would mean an improvement in terms of the economy on the economic side, on the educational side; it would mean we would go to a much higher rate of productivity per capita; it would mean a recovery from most of the things that we suffer from in recent times here.

So what we have to do: it would not be difficult to define a program which would represent a true pathway to recovery of the United States system. That could be done. It has not been done recently, but it can be done: Just simply take Franklin Roosevelt's policies. Now, these occurred under varying conditions, but what Franklin Roosevelt did, given the conditions under which he was operating, was good. It was excellent. It was a recovery, it was called a "recovery" then, the Franklin Roosevelt recovery.

# Furtwängler: The Baton Raised To Silence Tyranny

by Renée Sigerson

Aug. 23—When in October 2014, Lyndon La-Rouche launched the "Manhattan Project," igniting a process to create viable political leadership, and thereby to usher in the end of the Bush/Obama era of calamity, the personality of conductor Wilhelm Furtwängler, Germany's leading musician of the Twentieth Century, was incorporated as an integral component of the concept underlying this political campaign.

Furtwängler's oft-stated moral conviction was that the practice which deserves to be called music—namely, Classical music—is not based on "sound;" but, as the greatest composers of the Bach through Brahms period grasped, rather music is a *living* form of ideas, which comes to life only when evoked "between" and "behind" the notes composers write on a page. Furtwängler's legacy, his insistence that ideas reside "between" and not on objects, has now become a standard reference-point for those participating in the Manhattan Project, for developing the political process upon which the birth of a new form of political leadership must be generated.

To be precise: Politics must no longer be a laundry list of "issues," just as music is not a stream of notes. Political leadership has to be based on ordering principles, which situate legitimate human concerns under an evolving concept of *the true nature of the human species*, a guiding moral notion which Furtwängler embraced. The enemies of Furtwängler in the Congress for Cultural Freedom and other polluted, British-dominated channels during his lifetime recognized as much. In keeping with their intention never to allow such ideas to flourish, the London dictators of "artistic taste" sought to destroy Furtwängler by eliminating his influence from musical institutions worldwide.

societé wilhelm furtwängler

*Wilhelm Furtwängler (1886-1954) conducting the Berlin Philharmonic in 1938.*

Since his first encounter with Furtwängler under seemingly unlikely circumstances in 1946, (more below), Lyndon LaRouche has recognized in Furtwängler's unique success in musical performance a very special "effect"—that of igniting within audiences a hovering sense of genius acting upon the human mind. The ability to produce and sustain the poet's device of "ambiguity"—indefiniteness and precision at the same time—and to sustain with creative tension the unity of extended musical compositions, arouses within the mind of the citizen who has access to this standard of art, a personal experience of sustained participation in a process of creative discovery. To successfully navigate through the troubled waters of today's global war and economic disintegration, an assembly of politically active citizens who have shared this kind of intellectual and moral experience is desperately needed.

Today, for the United States to reverse its own economic and moral decline, and prevent such breakdown from being the trigger for thermonuclear holocaust, access to the quality of "genius"—insight rooted in compassion, and combined with a scientifically rigorous view of how to rebuild the economy—must become the standard for political dialogue.

Thus, the Manhattan Project, by combining great Classical music with political dialogue, becomes the inspiring element to overwhelm any morally corrupt, vaudeville-like charade which too often dominates what citizens are assaulted with as Presidential campaigning. Wherever the Presidential campaign does not descend into typical, media-driven forms of degeneracy, the influence of the higher principles the Manhattan Project embodies have, even at this preliminary stage, been a factor in elevating the political process to a sane plateau.

It is also the case that the time has come to make available forever a truthful portrayal of the life and mind of Wilhelm Furtwängler. The attacks launched against him after World War II among the Anglo-American and Hapsburg-related elite circles who not only despised him, but even feared him, have been a major factor in the onset of a morally weak and sickened environment in which Classical culture has been withering away. It is increasingly even drowning in the howling noise of demonic frenzy poured out by popular "entertainments" on electronic devices; and it is so weakened that no institution has yet existed which can effectively defend the extraordinary importance of Classical culture for mankind.

As LaRouche has correctly emphasized, since Furtwängler's performances of the conceptually challenging Franz Schubert "Great" Symphony No. 9 in C Major, recorded on several occasions between 1950 and 1954, there has never occurred anywhere in the world any comparable performance of a major symphonic work bequeathed by a great composer.

Study of this symphony, and of Furtwängler's delivery of it in the 1950s, is now an integral part of the political activities underway in Manhattan.

## Begin at the End

As in studying a musical composition, where it is useful to begin work from the concluding section, so discussion of "who was Wilhelm Furtwängler" is best presented by beginning with the last decade of his life. This situates the significance of his early development under the influence of circles participating in the European world of Chancellor Otto von Bismarck's Germany.

Imagine the tall and arthritic figure of Furtwängler standing in a row of personalities, made up of the people who salvaged and rebuilt war-torn Europe out of the vast rubble of World War II. Konrad Adenauer, West Germany's 14-year-long Chancellor until he retired at 87, is standing shoulder to shoulder with France's genius President Charles de Gaulle. Dwight Eisenhower and Douglas MacArthur are also in the row, in which Albert Einstein should also be included. Behind them, a new generation of leaders can also be seen, such as Africa's Kwame Nkrumah, and the founders (in 1961) of the Non-Aligned Movement, with the first signs of a Kennedy and Martin Luther King era being brought into existence with help from such older leaders of stature as Eleanor Roosevelt.

These are the peers of Wilhelm Furtwängler, and in comparison to them, he embodies the highest achievement of genius. They are typified by people who, despite the unparalleled horror of even the First World War, had never forfeited their optimistic certainty that humanity, as a species, can be improved upon to eliminate the causes of ever more violent orgies of destruction, and that a better purpose exists for mankind than marching to the imperial drumbeat of massive annihilation as the source for achieving power.

Like most of the people on that list, Furtwängler had to fight with great determination against the influence of the British Empire after World War II, to be allowed to lend his talents and gifts to heal the horrific wounds of the war. Even though the London financiers and the British aristocracy had played a huge role in imposing Hitler and Nazism upon post-World War I Germany, following the Axis's defeat, London reverted to the heavy-handed policy of once again blaming Germany and "German culture" for the maniacal Nazi movement and its strategic fascist war alliance. The coverup of the London-Wall Street role in nurturing the Austrian-born Hitler was massive. Everything was done to blame "the German mind-set," to cover for London's role in promoting the nihilistic Nazi gangs so similar to the forma-

# Shut Down Wall Street; It Just Blew Out!

*Below is an edited transcript of excerpts of Lyndon La-Rouche's Saturday, August 22, 2015 Dialogue with the Manhattan Project.*

**Dennis Speed:** My name is Dennis Speed, and on behalf of the LaRouche Political Action Committee I want to welcome everybody for our dialogue today with Lyndon LaRouche.

We always like to begin with making sure that everyone is properly oriented, and therefore I'd like to say that Barack Obama must be removed, as President of the United States. If you're in this meeting and you don't know that that's what the topic is, now you know. And it's not a topic because *it's* the topic. It's the topic because civilization is at stake, and we intend, as Americans, to invoke the principle of the American Presidency against the present interloper in the White House.

So we're going to get right into questions, and we're of course happy to have Lyn with us again this week; and we'd just like to take the first question, right away and start off.

Hello, Lyn. Earlier this week in the *New York Times* was placed an insert by a newspaper *Epoch Times*, which is a newspaper produced by the Falun Gong. They took up a very interesting subject and cited you on this question, which is the question of the Verdi tuning. It was a whole two-page insert on Aug. 14. The title is "Music Tuned To 432 Hz Said To Heal, Uplift." We'll flash an image of what the newspaper looks like, but I'm just going to read through a little bit of it and seek your comments on the matter.

> Now, let's take the case of New York City, which I think is of some relevance to what we're saying here, right? So what are we going to do? I would say, what we should do summarily, is shut down Wall Street. Because Wall Street is about to blow! And there's nothing that can prevent Wall Street from blowing, except by shutting it down. If we wait for it to blow, it will blow out the entire economy—with chaos!

It begins: "A decades-long debate among musicians about tuning is bound up with Nazi conspiracy theories, New Age healing methods, practical consideration of what's easiest on a singer's vocal chords, a revived connection to ancient math and aesthetics, and more abstract connections to a higher order.

"Should instruments be tuned to 440 hertz or 432 hertz?

## The Verdi Tuning

"In 1955, an international standard of A=440 hertz was set to unify the different concert pitches previously in use. This means the number of vibrations per second of the middle A is 440. But some say A=432 hertz brings music to another level."

So, the article cites studies that have been done where listeners who were tested listening to both the higher Nazi/Goebbels tuning and the Verdi tuning, almost overwhelmingly prefer the lower Verdi tuning, saying that the 440 tuning is "uncomfortable, oppressive, narrow minded." They think that the lower tuning is "peaceful and calm."

Later in the article they cite Luciano Pavarotti, Renata Tebaldi, the professional Italian opera singers, as preferring the lower tuning, and then it goes on: "Was 440Hz Tuning a Nazi Initiative?" And they go through some of that question, including, they say: "Laurent Rosenfeld wrote the article 'How the Nazis Ruined Musical Tuning,' published in the September 1988 edition of the magazine *Executive Intelligence Review* (a publication associated with the LaRouche movement, known to have some controversial political stances)."

And then they examine the question of the Nazis' preference for the higher tuning, and then the rest of the article looks at why the lower tuning might be preferable for water molecules and some numerological questions, but it's certainly striking. This insert, this *New York Times* insert, was brought to our attention by a conductor friend of ours. And in the context of the Manhattan project you initiated last October, the chorus that we've been building since December, all of which highlighting this lower tuning, I think it would be useful to get your comments. Thank you.

**Lyndon LaRouche:** Well, this is something we've had a big fight about and I've been part of this big fight. I'm not a musician as such, but I have had very close relationships with the greatest musicians living, in my life time; most of them in Italy and other locations and to some degree in New York City, in the same time period. This standard is not one of some arbitrary figure. It's a recognition of a musical value which is implicitly required by competent, shall we say, competent musical performance, and therefore the development of the ability to reach the expression that this demands is really a standard for defining everything that's important about music, especially Classical music.

## What are Human Principles?

And this is something that belongs to mankind, it belongs to the best forces of mankind. And anything that's different than that on the basis of history, the effects of history, was a failure. And of course, we often use, as I did, the Italian standard, and the Italian standard is a true standard, and we stick to it.

And that's something which people have to learn from experience by meeting that standard. And when they are able to meet that standard and compare it with some other opportunity than their own singing, this leads them into understand the true meaning of what Classical musical composition represents. It is not an arbitrary scheme. It is not a gimmick. It's a natural development of the human singing voice, and the singing voice is the proper background for the expression of all artistic expression of any kind; and if you want to make a public speech on an issue, it should be in those terms of reference. If you do that, you'll find that your mental capabilities will be strengthened. Whereas if you don't do that, your mental capabilities may be reduced. So, I would advise you to accept the Verdi standard.

**Q:** I'm J— and I'm with Lynn Yen and the Foundation for the Revival of Classical Culture, and I'm going to be honest, that I had many questions before I came

Movisol

*The Verdi standard: Italian opera singer Antonella Banaudi gives a singing lesson, showing how the tone should be placed from the top of the head.*

here. But standing here, it really takes away my breath. I guess I'm just going to keep this short and simple.

Within these past two years, studying with Miss Yen and learning about the Kepler nested solids and learning about the relationship between music and education, it's really opened my eyes to the education system today. In the high school that I go to and in many other high schools in New York City, they are starting to cut the music programs in to save money, so they can hire new and younger teachers; so they can replace the old ones and pay them cheaper.

So I was wondering if there was anything I or anyone else that goes to Miss Yen's program could do, to basically help spread the word and also keep music programs alive and show the importance of how music and education go together well. Thank you.

**LaRouche:** The answer to the implicit question, is that there is a certain set of values, which are consistent with Classical musical composition and performance. These are not however arbitrary standards in any sense. They are things which have emerged as adopted on the basis of understanding what the human mind requires, in order to express humanity.

In other words, the problem we have, is, what is human? What are human principles? Don't they have to imply the quality of principles which actually fits the requirements of design of the human mind? In other words, these are not arbitrary values. They're values which have come to be understood by those who experienced states of mind, mental states of mind; and people can recognize eventually by experience what states of mind, including tuning, of expression are required to meet the standard required for the *principle of human mental life*.

And therefore, we want people to be able find coherence between understanding music and understanding the principle of the human mind. And it's that coherence which is crucial. And all the greatest musicians have been able to induce most people to recognize that distinction, and the principles that embodies. And Verdi is an excellent particular selection. And Verdi and his work is, still, an up-to-date standard for understanding the meaning of both music and musical composition.

## The Strategic Defense Initiative

**Q:** Good afternoon. I've been following your teaching for a number of years, and one of the things I've learned how to do is view things from a big-picture, top-down perspective. And in that regard, I find it easy to view everything that's going on as a battle of good versus evil. Most people are somewhere in the middle, but on the one hand, you have a bunch of very rich, therefore powerful people, like the Bushes.

I used to think you were a Bush basher, and then the more I learned about them I kind of think you were kind of easy on them. You talk about Prescott Bush a lot, but one thing you don't mention a lot is his son, who I found out was fairly integral in the assassination of JFK. He gets rewarded with being President and one, if not two (hopefully not), of his sons end up becoming President as well.

I'm a registered Republican—and now we have Donald Trump, and I am trying to decide where he is on the spectrum of good or evil. I kind of want him to be on the side of good, but I noticed right from the get-go you're very dead set against him. I'm thinking he's either somewhere between an irritant who's out to fracture the Republican Party, which they seem to do fairly well on their own; or people have been calling him Reaganesque, and I'm like, well…. But I would think if he was Reaganesque, you don't necessarily dislike him because he's a Republican. If he was Reaganesque, I've got to believe that that would at least give him the benefit of the doubt.

I've heard a lot recently about end-times philosophy and prophecy. And so in regards to where Donald Trump falls in this, I don't know—my question is: Is it possible that Donald Trump is the anti-Christ? [laughter]

**LaRouche:** Well, Trump is—let's take two parts of this. Let's get the garbage out of the way first. When we remove the garbage, then we'll look at the content of what the garbage has overcome.

First of all, I think a recommendation should be for reference, should be a political one. And now I had the good fortune to be recruited in the late 1970s, recruited by what was going to become the Reagan Administration. And I was specially trained and rehearsed in methods for dealing with the physical principles of science, in what Reagan had intended to be; and I was put in charge of a major operation, which involved international systems of combat and avoidance of combat. This was my assignment.

I was also brought into an operation, where I met with the leadership of the Russian-Soviet system at that time, what was left of it; and we came to an agreement to ensure that there would be no warfare between the United States, and what had been the Soviet Union, the relics of the Soviet Union. And I'd been in charge of that operation, which was the SDI, the Strategic Defense Initiative, which was my particular project. I operated together with many people associated with the back room of the intelligence service of the President.

This is my experience. And I regret very much that we lost him, our President—that is, he was assassinated, virtually. He survived. He was a physically tough guy and he survived physically, but it was an attempted assassination, by people who were related to the Bush family. And therefore, that assassination attack on him weakened the President, Ronald Reagan, physically, and therefore other forces moved in on his Presidency and began to contaminate it, despite his noble efforts at the time.

After that point we had Bill Clinton, who tried to be a great President, and Bill was not a perfect President, but he was a very useful one relative to the alternatives. And after that, after Bill Clinton left office, there has been nothing but crap in the Presidential system. There are individuals in the Presidential system who are honest people and so forth, but the ruling force in the Presidential systems since that time, has been the worst possible crap, and Barack Obama is the crappiest of them all, and the most dangerous.

## Hillary Was a Patsy

**Q:** This is A—. Earlier this week two articles appeared in various publications, one in the *Washington Times*. Both were addressing the Hillary Clinton situation, as it stands. The one from the *Washington Times* begins by saying, "Ms. Clinton is careening toward possible criminal charges involving her alleged mis-

*Senator Birch Bayh (above) (D-Ind, 1963-1981) and Representative Emanuel Celler (D-NY, 1923-1973) co-authored the 25th Amendment in 1967.*

handling of classified materials over her personal server and President Obama is driving the bus." The second one, I think it's something online, from someone people familiar with this organization know, where they quote Dick Morris, the famous toe sucker, extensively. "From the Clinton point of view this was all set up by Obama, Michelle, and Valerie Jarrett, the three of them. Barack hates Bill, Valerie and Michelle hate Hillary," and here it starts out—here's a new one— "Hillary Clinton is planning to start blaming Barack Obama from her own personal emails." [quotes as read]

Now it was, I don't remember exactly when, but you were the first one to say what is required for Hillary Clinton to both be patriotic, save the nation, and herself, in a sense; while her Presidential hopes have been dashed, since her failure or exposure on Glass-Steagall, we have these developments now, and obviously these people can be writing and their articles go on with their own bent, but I was wondering what you could say to us now on Hillary Clinton and these matters.

**LaRouche:** Well, Hillary Clinton was a patsy. She had had certain talents, certain recognizable talents, but she came under the thumb of a brutish animal called Barack Obama. This whole crisis about that came to a climax, where Obama had committed a fraud in terms of his own cupidity, in dealing with the assassinations of at least three or more individuals in the U.S. intelligence/diplomatic service. So the issue came up. He had lied—the President had—and said that this was an offense, an insult to the cause of the Saudi religion. There was no truth to that whatsoever.

It was Obama, himself, who organized the set-up which resulted in the assassination of at least three, or probably four, officials of the United States government. She [Hillary] had been subjected to the fact that he had done this, and that Hillary was carrying the load for him. And at first she made a stab at exposing the President, Obama. Now Obama was the one who was guilty of all the crimes committed against the citizens of the United States, the official citizens of the United States in that area, and Obama *lied.* Also Obama had a bunch of women who were working for him, and they lied, too.

### The 25th Amendment

Now the situation today is that Hillary Clinton knows, and has direct knowledge of the lies by Barack Obama. She could have sunk him them. She could have testified then, and he would've been out of the Presidency automatically. He, however, is a threatening person. He's a madman, himself. He intimidated the hell out of her, and she backed off and refused to state the fact that she personally knew, and she had identified. But when it came to the conflict with Obama, she capitulated; and to this day, she has continued to capitulate to Obama's threats and brutality.

Now, the obvious thing here, is that if Hillary Clinton would tell the truth, the truth which we know she had against Obama, she would be in danger from Obama, because he's a killer. Obama's step-father was a killer. He was in a different part of the planet at that time. But he was a killer; he was known as a killer. The mother was a bad person, but she was a weakling, who didn't have the guts to stand up to her husband. but Obama is the child of his own step-father, in that way.

So if we are going to have a United States, if we are not going to have a thermonuclear war, if we are not going have a collapse of the world through the launching of a thermonuclear war, which *the Obama Administration now represents as an immediate threat*, that's the problem to be considered. And those who have the guts and knowledge to expose this, or contribute to exposing it, really have in their hands the possibility of

> **Obama must be removed from the Presidency under the 25th Amendment, and it must be done quickly, now. And that will clean the whole thing up. Put him in the jug. Throw him out of office, according to the 25th Amendment. That's the solution.**

saving this nation and other nations from a gross extermination through thermonuclear warfare, even in this month or the next month. We don't know which is the closest, but it's on now.

*Obama must be removed from the Presidency under the 25th Amendment, and it must be done quickly, now.* And that will clean the whole thing up. Put him in the jug. Throw him out of office, according to the 25th Amendment. That's the solution.

## Mankind is a Unique Species

**Q:** Hi, Mr. LaRouche, this is E— from the Bronx, New York City. I agree with you 100% when you say that man is not an animal. He's creative, and he's trying to discover universal principles or laws of the universe. But I believe that biologically we have to say that man is part of the animal kingdom, but he's the highest form of animal on Earth. He has a mind; he can think; he can rationalize.

All animals operate by brains. We do, too, but we have minds, and so we can think. The lower animals, like the lions, tigers, horses, whatever, they do not know that they are living in a universe, that they are living on a planet. They just operate according to the jungle law of eat, kill, devour, and so on, but man is higher than that....

**LaRouche:** OK. I know the difference of mankind from an animal. Mankind is not an animal. And no animal is mankind. This is a unique character, because the characteristic is located where? It's located in the powers of creativity. Those powers of creativity which no animal has—no form of animal has ever manifest such skills.

Now the problem comes up on the other side. The problem is that we have often societies, and forms of societies, human societies, which are degenerate; that is, they should be human, but they're not, in their behavior. And therefore, we have to make that distinction.

The power of creativity, for example, the discovery by Kepler of the Solar System: Kepler, by himself, was the genius who discovered the *principle* of the Solar System. Implicitly the same thing is extended to a higher level, the Galactic System. For example, most of the water that mankind depends upon depends upon the Galaxy, not an inferior system. So that when we operate in this way with true physical science, with the greatest scientists, and all greatest scientists show these charac-

*"Saint Jerome Reading in an Italian Landscape," by Rembrandt Harmensz van Rijn, an etching done in 1653.*

teristics; and only the stupid people, people who are ignorant on these things, or they're stupefied....

For example, what's frightening is the education system of the people of the United States. Now there are some rare institutions, in which the teaching is intelligent, and Manhattan used to be one of the places where the better quality of education in schools occurred. Most of the rest of the world has been rather defective in this front, in this prospect. There are things in Europe, parts of Europe, which have highly developed mental life, human mental life. Einstein, for example, is the paragon. Einstein was the unique figure in his own existence, and no one really recently has managed to compare with that.

So anyway, these are the things. Mankind is a unique species, and the Christian religion, for example, is absolutely correct on this point: Mankind is not an animal. Mankind depends upon the service of animals, that animals who adapt to human beings are useful to human beings. In that respect they have a very significant role in life. But mankind, the human mind is a unique phenomenon, for which so far, we have never discovered another, except humanity as such. Mankind is not perfect, because mankind has not perfected.

For example, the purpose of true education is to enable mankind, people, to not only become more intelligent, more skilled, but to also get to another higher level, the same level which is characteristic of Albert Einstein; Einstein's genius was a very specific quality of true genius, as opposed to a lot of other people who were very skilled, but they were not geniuses. And what we do want, we do want to have geniuses. But geniuses are only a particular type of development of human beings; animals are not geniuses.

## The New Presidency

**Q:** Good afternoon, Mr. LaRouche. My name is E—, and I currently reside in Wilmington, Delaware, but I was born in Paterson, New Jersey, which is where Alexander Hamilton kicked off an industrial revolution in this country. And now we're badly in need of this kind of policy, this kind of idea.

Well, I understand that there are some people in the Democratic Party that are running for President, and we don't want to have an evolutionary battle between different beasts. What we're trying to do is create a Presidency which you suggested the policies that it should be oriented around, and the former governor of Maryland, Mr. O'Malley, he's circling the circuit now for Presidential campaign. And he's going to show his face in Philadelphia, and I think it's incumbent on myself to do something to make sure that he gets your message, directly, and I would volunteer to do that next week, or in a week or two, but I would like you to give a succinct notion of what exactly we need to inform his campaign, to move so that the Democratic Party can actually be revived to represent the people of this country.

**LaRouche:** Mm-hmm, OK. I can answer that. First of all, O'Malley is one of the people who I would tend to support for candidacy for the Presidency now; it goes as much by default as anything else, that O'Malley is one of the people who probably would be on the safe side of being a choice for President. I'm not fully aware of all the details of that, I don't know the intimate secrets of his life and so forth; but I would say, yes, he's near the top of the list of candidates for designation as President.

Now, the question is, what's the answer to this whole process? Well, first of all, *a* President, a single President

by himself, is not a security for a successful Presidency. The closest we got to that was people like Abraham Lincoln, and so forth, and Franklin Roosevelt. These were nearly perfect Presidents, for the purposes of being Presidents; and there were a few others who also fit. I could go through that, but let's not bother with that right now.

The point here is that we have to have a conception of policy, that we have to have a Presidential appointee, who is surrounded by a team, a team of skilled people who as a team are a relative guarantee of a successful President. Now, I think that Obama has to be removed immediately, obviously. I think O'Malley is one of the people who should be considered a candidate for the appointment to the Presidency.

But what I'm really looking for, is for a team which fills out a Presidential office, a team which by itself will not only be good, and the President must not only be good, but he could be assassinated or he could die. Therefore, this makes us aware that we must have a Presiden*cy*, that is, a team of people who work together to fulfill the office of President, that is, the functional office of the Presidents for the United States.

We need a team, we need a selection of people, who are qualified to assemble around a chosen President as a candidate, and that we must rely upon the working and development and support of that Presiden*cy*, as the leading edge to the solutions which we most desperately desire right now.

**Q:** [follow-up] Thank you very much. One more follow-up. Do you think I should urge him to get the United States to join the BRICS and start campaigning on that, or just stick to what he's doing with Glass-Steagall, or how do you think—what would you say to him if you were there?

**LaRouche:** I would suggest that you may be a prospective member of a team of people who are going to deal with exactly that problem. In other words, what we need is a rallying of people of obvious competence, and obvious principle; we need them to run for position in association with a new President. We need to form a committee, which is not only a formal part of the Presidential system, but a periphery of people who support the Presidential system, and influence him. You need the kind of unification of leading figures in society, who understand the problem, who can recognize one another as sharing the same concern; have a core which is the service of the government itself, but also people who can be turned to for help *to* the President, the Presidency, and reciprocally, accept that.

Because you've got to have a whole system which is capable of recognizing the high variety of requirements of a Presidency of this type, at this kind of time. We need a very finely developed Presidential system. We also need a close relationship between ordinary citizens, who qualify as being advisors to the Presidential system. And these are people who can help us, help the Presidential system, by saying "Hey, I'm here. This is what my suggestion is." And this means, like engineering policies, engineering projects, all these kinds of things which can be done either by government, or can be done by official skills outside of government, but who are all really part of the same process that the government represents.

## Mankind's Quality of Genius

**Q:** Hello, my name is L— and I'm a retired licensed architect, and I have a question regarding the profession of architecture, and then the construction industry as related to society, and compensation, as a kind of representation of the way we're going as a society. What I'm trying to say is, as a licensed architect for 34 years, I earned less on an hourly basis as a consultant to various offices; I was earning less or luckily the same amount as a plumber or an electrician, or a master mason. And so, my question is, if the education is not respected, where are we going as a society? What are we....?

**LaRouche:** OK, you asked a question, and I'm going to give you an answer, which may surprise you; or you may enjoy it.

Look, the problem we have is that at the end of the Nineteenth Century in the United States, we had a few great principal minds, great leaders, great scientists; but at the same time, at the end of that period, what happened was a terrible experiment, a terrible experience as well: What happened is, suddenly the great scientists were being pushed aside, and fakers, you know, scientists who were fakers, the fakers began to take over. And they took over under Bertrand Russell, who was a very evil man; he was successful as being very evil, and even the sound of his name is the name of evil to this present day.

So what happened in the Twentieth Century, when we got out of '1890s into the Twentieth Century, there was an accelerated rate of destruction of science in the United States. Now some people were still practicing science in that Twentieth Century. *But! But!* very few

were actually competent in science. What they practiced was arithmetic, mathematics, and mathematics is not science. Science is more profound, and Einstein, for example, in the Twentieth Century was the exemplar of science. His discoveries were *amazing* to all who observed.

Now, we're coming to a period where we have very poor education in the school system. We had, in a former time, teachers and so forth who were very skilled; but over the course of time, there has been a decay, a degenerative process, in the educational policies and practices of the United States and European nations, as well. There are some exceptions to that, but they're very minimal.

Therefore, what we need is to concentrate on understanding what the principle is, and the principle is this: The principle is that mankind has a quality of genius which is unique to the human mind, and it's the development of that thing, typified by the accomplishment of Einstein; Einstein is the measure of this, and during that century there were a lot of good scientists, who did good things, but they had problems, because they swallowed up things like crap artists in science. In what was taught in universities; the universities in most cases, what they were teaching as science, was actually crap. It was pragmatic stuff. And Einstein was unique. He made no crap. He made only science.

## China is Way Ahead

Now, there were other people who were not fully talented; they were not true scientists, but they wished to be scientists. They wished the goal of being scientists, and they made some good efforts in that direction; they made improvements, contributed important improvements. But that process has been diminishing. How many people do you have who are still competent, in this generation? Since the process of degeneration of culture in the United States, has been dropping ever since, the beginning of the Twentieth Century.

And it's accelerated. Now, look at what we've got in the school systems; look at what we've got on the streets in terms of personnel. We do not have a body of competently educated and trained people; we have *some* people, who have *some* talent, more or less. But look at our youth, our young people now—in this century, present, uncompleted century, is *destructive*. It's killing us!

And therefore, what we have to do, we have to say, what you're talking about, yes! What you have to do in this case is find out ways in which we can bring true science, and what that means, into practice, and those who

WWW.NEWS.CN

Hsinhua/Jin Liwang

*A photo taken on July 27, 2015 of what will be the world's largest radio telescope, located in the Chinese mountains of Guizhou, when it's completed in 2016.*

had some education; most of them were illiterate, right? So... [crosstalk] I don't think that's a good example. I mean, China, in fact, they're starting to slow down just because of that, because it's not really a mass educated society, as for example, the American society is, or the European societies are.

**LaRouche:** I think China has a higher quality of scientific achievement now than does the United States. That's a fact. This is a surge which occurred in terms of the history of China, which comes under actually the impetus of the new government, the present government in China. And the progress of China, for example, in space, in terms of the Solar System things, China's way ahead, of the rest of the world on these issues.

And what's developing in China,—China has characteristic problems; they're left over from earlier times, from the earlier kind of system. But China is making very significant progress, and it's working very closely with Russia, very close with India, very close with other parts of the planet. You'll find what's called the BRICS phenomenon in South America. We have the comparable things in some parts of South Africa; we have other things like that that are there.

The greatest problems are concentrated, in the trans-Atlantic community; the trans-Atlantic community is the most rapidly degenerating part of the whole planetary system right now. There are some other things which are leftover degeneracy.

But this is what we're dealing with. And we can win because humanity can become contagious; science can become contagious. And our job is to make sure that science becomes contagious, from the educational system, all the way up and down. And then you'll get an effect you would like.

can do it even imperfectly are needed. Because if you look at the population of our children in the education system, you know we're in a desperate situation, and it's going to take almost a miracle, to get us out of this mess.

**Q:** [follow-up] Yes, but also the media is not helping at all, where more or less, all of the society is a prisoner and dependent on the media, and the media are just encouraging superficiality. I mean, whoever gets to sing better and to jump around better, is appreciated than development of humankind

**LaRouche:** Of course! That's the disease! *That* is the disease we have. And what we're doing, with a few people who really are not subscribing to that disease, we are depending upon *them* to revive a quality of leadership, and they come from all kinds of quarters of life. They're too few, but those are there who represent, really, the opportunity for mankind of recovery.

This is global. We have to take into consideration, the best of what China's doing today, and China's the most advanced nation in terms of economy; that is, in terms of science.

**Q:** [follow-up] Sorry, but from a social point of view, China, less than 100 years ago was a feudal state, right? I mean, 100 years ago, the beginning of the Twentieth Century, they were really peasants, OK? With 1% that

### The New York Schools

**Q:** Good afternoon, Mr. LaRouche. This is J— from Brooklyn, New York. I appreciate everything that you said to the last two or three speakers, because as you know, I am a teacher and I do teach science in middle school; and I'm not exactly sure how to put my question, but I want you to hear what I have to say about this particular subject:

We have a paper called *The Teacher*, and it comes out usually in September, after the summer where students and teachers are off. Well, this one is a special issue that came out in August. And what's interesting about this is that the AFT [American Federation of Teachers], which is the parent organization for the UFT, the United Federation of Teachers [in New York], has endorsed Hillary Clinton for President in the 2016 election.

Now, the AFT has 1.6 *million* members, as I said; it is the parent organization of the UFT. They say in this article where they have endorsed Hillary, that she has "vision, experience, and leadership." [AFT President] Randi Weingarten says that Clinton said during an AFT interview that she had with Ms. Clinton—"it's just dead wrong to make teachers scapegoats. Where I come from, teachers are the solution not, the problem, and I strongly believe unions are part of that solution, too."

Now, Hillary seems to have made a lot of statements at some convention that took place between teachers from the UFT and teachers from the AFT, that was held in Washington in July. Now—I wasn't invited to that convention.... [LaRouche laughs] So now, this newspaper says, that because of these interviews with different candidates and everything, they decided to endorse Hillary.

I know what I want to do when school actually starts, and to me, this is kind of a sneaky little thing that they did over the summer, when they have the *real* assembly of delegates, of which I am one. I know what I need to do when that meeting occurs in early September, right after school starts. However, for others who are in the audience, and who might belong to unions because there are so many thousands of unions in the United States, and they probably will be coming out and endorsing Hillary and other really bad people for the Presidential election, I would like you to comment on, first of all,—also Randi Weingarten is a *known* Wall Street agent; we already know that. She's friends with [former mayor Michael] Bloomberg, and he was a horror.

So, with that in mind, how would you comment on how we should handle these types of endorsements? I love what you said about the Presiden*cy* being a group, a committee, an actual team of members to run the Presidency; and how can we get that across to our union members, when these endorsements and these things

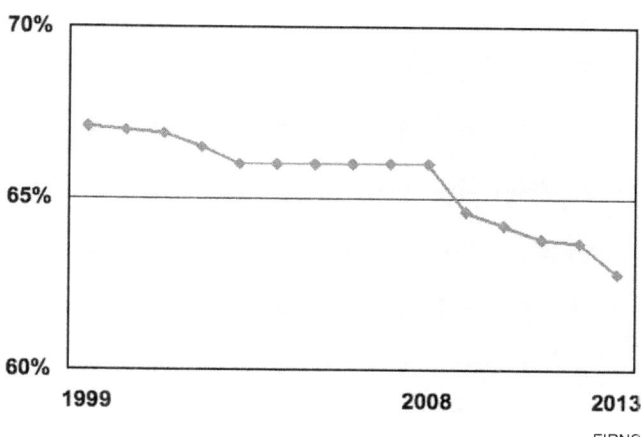

FIGURE 1
**Labor Participation Rate**
(percentage)

EIRNS

*The collapse of the labor participation rate is a measure of hidden unemployment in the U.S. economy.*

arise, especially like this little sneaky thing that happened over the summer?

**LaRouche:** Yeah, well, that's a problem we have to combat; we all have to combat it. Because you can't just stay with teachers or something like; you can't with just one category, you've got to take a broad category; and since you are the kind of teacher you are, in terms of the way you function, you don't have a problem with being yourself. But you may have a problem with some people who don't quite understand what you're trying to do. And therefore, it's just sort of automatic. If you come in with this kind of thing and talk to me in this way, what do you think my reaction is? I'm elated that you exist. [laughter] And I'm right! It's a good judgment.

No, we know that in Manhattan school systems, there were leading teachers, teachers prominent within the institution, and these teachers are the backbone, or *were* the backbone in former times, of the education system in New York City. And the whole thing, the whole thing within that direction, the universities, the teaching schools and so forth, were all of that nature. What has happened is, we've had a degeneration in the quality of life, in terms of education, in terms of practices which bear on education, and the conditions of life of our citizens, it's *horrible*.

### Hillary's Only Weapon

If you take the percentile of the population of the United States which are eligible to be active, employed citizens, who ain't employed! The great mass of unemployed, qualified employees is missing! And this thing is a disease, and therefore we have to fight this thing; we have to fight this out.

Now on the Hillary thing, just to complete the circle: Hillary was a person of a certain talent with whom I had respectable relations, when she was actively married to her husband. And then she went out on her own, and she got in over her head. And she got an ego going to match the problems. And she's still got certain values, a residue of what she was able to do beforehand.

---

**We have to say, okay. She made a lot of mistakes; all right, so what? She's still human, right? She made mistakes. What she has to do now is make an un-mistake, and that means to identify the evidence she has against Obama himself. Because he's going to kill her, if he can. And she'd better get him out of office while she can.**

---

I saw her go into service under Obama, and I knew that was wrong. She shouldn't have done it, because he was going to ruin her. And he has gone pretty far to ruin her. He's trying to kill her, practically, right now! All the efforts are being expended *against her*, now! And the source of that is Obama! Obama's the one who's out to destroy her, personally!

Now, she has one weapon which I emphasize everywhere: That she knows, and has the proof, that Obama was an evil, lying bastard, and that she caved into his pressure, his intimidation, and she told a lie! Now, here she is, he's trying to get rid of her: I would say, fairly, he would not be displeased if she were to die, suddenly. I don't know how that would work out, but I see in that direction it's very clear.

I would say: We have to say, OK, she made a lot of mistakes; all right, so what? She's still human, right? She made mistakes. What she has to do now is make an *un*-mistake, and that means to identify the evidence she has against Obama himself. Because he's going to kill her, if he can. And she'd better get him out of office while she can.

**Q:** [follow-up] Well, we can. Thank you! [applause]

**Q:** Hi, Mr. LaRouche, this is R— from Bergen County, New Jersey. Talking about the degeneracy of the quality of life, and also having to do with the educa-

tion system, one example is the massive growth in student loans, which I've taken a look at recently: I want to use that as an example, to make an overall more general point, and then ask you my question based on that.

The student loans have become astronomical: Millions of students now have loans in the order of $100,000 or more. So talk about degenerating the quality of life; students get out of colleges, with this expensive, low-grade education. If they manage to get a job, they can barely survive, because virtually all of their income is going to pay off their loans. So it's quite usual these days for post-college students to be living at home, because they simply can't afford to rent a place, and that completely disrupts....

I mean, many of these students, having something like a $125,000 in loans will *never* pay them off. They're going to go through the rest of their life paying these loans. And the size of this bubble, the size of these loans, is pretty big; it's huge at this point, it's something on the order of a trillion. Something like 14% of these students have simply stopped paying. They're not paying the loans off. That's one example of the type of thing that is going on.

Another example I note—and it really concerns me—is the deterioration of the currency exchange rates: I'm looking at a report from the *Wall Street Journal*. Since the beginning of 2014, South Africa versus the dollar, down 14%; New Zealand versus the dollar, down 20%; Malaysian ringgit versus the dollar, down 20%; Brazil real down 31%; Canadian dollar down 16%. These are all primarily commodity-producing countries, so each of these countries has their own, specialized commodity that they export. We also know the case of oil breaking $40/barrel.

When I looked at all this information, first of all, it looks to me like this thing is in a death-spiral. I mean, it's just getting sucked down. Secondly, it reminded me of a model you developed some years ago, called "The Triple Curve," ["A Typical Collapse Function"], where, if I understand it correctly, your Triple Curve model stated that what will happen in a non-Glass-Steagall environment is that the amount of financial paper being issued will explode, and along with that, at the same time, the productivity level will drop.

Now, as I recall from that curve, there's a stable period, initially, then the two curves start to deviate; and then they deviate and they completely collapse in different directions. Productivity basically goes to negative infinity and the amount of paper goes up to positive in-

So therefore we have to get rid of it. That means we have to cancel Wall Street, because it must not be allowed to walk away with anything. It doesn't own anything, really. So therefore, what we have to do, is go back to the Glass-Steagall law of Franklin Roosevelt, put that into effect as national law, and you will automatically eliminate all the waste speculation. Kill it! Which is, you know,—Franklin Roosevelt intended to move in that direction, and did. I'm saying now, what is required is that the President of the United States must now shut down Wall Street, because it has no real value in it.

Therefore, since it has no real value, we should remove it; by doing so, we will eliminate a mass of debts, including the phony kinds of debts which went through the education system, trying to buy the students up.

finity. I suppose at that point, you have a state of complete meltdown of the global economy.

That's the situation I see happening at this point: Could you comment on that?

**Cancel Wall Street**

LaRouche: Yes, I can. I wrote the book on this thing, as you probably know. What happened is, I did this Triple Curve operation as a warning of what was threatened. Now, that meant that at a certain point, where these speculators were speculators, the speculation was going to show itself for what it is, and that has happened with aces, completely.

So what we have, is we have a complete decline in the productivity per capita of employed people, and people who should be employed but who unfortunately are not employed. And so, since that point, which came at the end of the Reagan Administration, it actually started under the Bush influence, in the Reagan Administration; and this was an accelerating rate of degeneration, which Wall Street really did; it was Wall Street as such which really did the job. And what they did, is they went down into a curve, which has gone down and down and down.

Now, the solution is—because that's what your statement poses; what's the question? What's the answer?

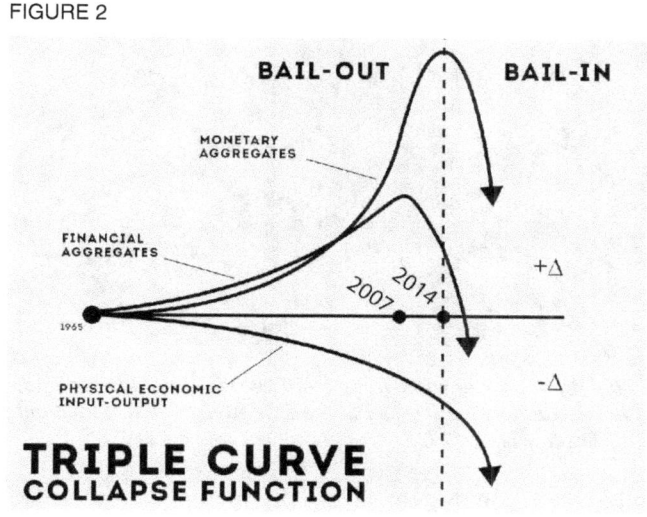

FIGURE 2

BAIL-OUT BAIL-IN

MONETARY AGGREGATES

FINANCIAL AGGREGATES

1965

2007 2014

+Δ

-Δ

PHYSICAL ECONOMIC INPUT-OUTPUT

**TRIPLE CURVE COLLAPSE FUNCTION**

EIRNS

*Lyndon LaRouche's Triple Curve function, updated to show the financial as well as economic collapse.*

The answer is, essentially, we shut down Wall Street. We don't pay it off, we shut it down. Now, on what pretext do we shut it down? The fact that it's bankrupt, it's hopelessly bankrupt. It's a bankruptcy which can never be bailed out. So what do we do? We simply cancel it.

Now, let's take the case of New York City, which I think is of some relevance to what we're saying here, right? So what are we going to do? I would say, what we should do summarily, is shut down Wall Street. Because Wall Street is about to blow! And there's nothing that can prevent Wall Street from blowing, except by shutting it down. If we wait for it to blow, it will blow out the entire economy—with chaos!

So therefore we have to get rid of it. That means we have to cancel Wall Street, because it must not be allowed to walk away with anything. It doesn't own anything, really. So therefore, what we have to do, is go back to the Glass-Steagall law of Franklin Roosevelt, put that into effect as national law, and you will automatically eliminate all the waste speculation. Kill it! Which is, you know,—Franklin Roosevelt intended to move in that direction, and did. I'm saying now, what is required is that the President of the United States must now *shut down Wall Street*, because *it has no real value in it.*

So we simply cancel that stuff, and go back to a Franklin Roosevelt style of Glass-Steagall law, with all the implications implicit in his law; that means shutting down all of these things, which ain't worth a penny anyway! And we have to then have a credit system established, as Franklin Roosevelt would have done, in that case, where we give credit to productive employment. We have to give subsidies and so forth to get people back on the payroll, and into productive employment. We have to build up educational systems which provide that kind of service, where we can get people who have lost skills, get them back into business. And that's what we have to do, now.

Therefore, since it has no real value, we should remove it; by doing so, we will eliminate a mass of debts, including the phony kinds of debts which went through the education system, trying to buy the students up.

So we simply cancel that stuff, and go back to a Franklin Roosevelt style of Glass-Steagall law, with all the implications implicit in his law; that means shutting down all of these things, which ain't worth a penny anyway! And we have to then have a credit system established, as Franklin Roosevelt would have done, in that case, where we give credit to productive employment. We have to give subsidies and so forth to get people back on the payroll, and into productive employment. We have to build up educational systems which provide that kind of service, where we can get people who have lost skills, get them back into business. And that's what we have to do, now.

Library of Congress
*Franklin Roosevelt with Harry Hopkins, his close adviser, and administrator of the Works Progress Administration, which put millions to work in 1933. This photo was taken in 1938.*

**Q:** [follow-up] So, there are elements who want to pretend that certain issues don't exist; it seems that the Congress wants to pretend that the Glass-Steagall issue simply doesn't exist: they don't want to hear about it, they don't want to know about it, it never existed, I don't know what you're talking about; it can't be done.

In doing so, is it correct to conclude that with this huge downdraft that's come and that we're in the middle of in this economy, that by doing that, the Congress is implicitly or explicitly shifting the liability of this crash onto the backs of the American people?

**LaRouche:** I think that's true in a sense, but I don't think it's the meaningful truth in the sense: Look, what you've got is, you've got a system which has had four terms of office essentially—Obama has not completed his second term of office, and between him and the Bush family before him—what you've got is a destruction of the U.S. economy, a destruction of everything that belongs to the name of U.S. productivity. And the skill levels are horrible! Why are the skill levels horrible? Because nobody is providing competently skilled employment.

The first thing you have to do in an economy is you have to build up the skills of employment; and you have to apply them to really meaningful things, you know, the thing I've spent a good deal of my life doing, on this kind of thing.

So that has to be done. And my optimism comes, in the fact that I think I have the medicine, which if adequately circulated, would sink this whole system. And right now, the thing is, we have to get Obama out of the picture.

### Get People Back to Work

Now, the Obama thing has two aspects to it: If you proceed properly, in terms of the hyperinflation which has been induced in a peculiar way, in terms of the U.S. economy in particular, then you're going to sink practically everything that's current money. So therefore, what you're going to have to do, is realize that all the so-called lost current money, is not really a lost current money; it's a loss which never really existed. Therefore, we have to proceed ruthlessly by a stronger dose of Franklin Roosevelt's policy in his Presidency: We have to *shut this thing down* and put people *back to work*, by selecting programs which may not be too productive, but we have to get the people back to work. We have to get them into employment; we have to help give them the skills they will need to carry them through this kind of employment. We did that kind of thing, under Franklin Roosevelt. We took people and bailed them out, with the WPA and PWA and so forth; we bailed them out! But it paid off: we'd have lost World War II if we hadn't done that!

And so therefore the time has come, where we have to pay attention. We're cutting out all the looting from Wall Street. Wall Street, you are cancelled. All you have to do, is do one thing, recognize that Wall Street, *right now, is hopelessly bankrupt*! You cannot get a penny out of Wall Street, not really, not a penny!

Now, think about Wall Street, and Manhattan. Think about all those wonderful skyscrapers, or sky scratchers, if you want to call them; and you say, "what are we going to do with all this rubbish?" All these buildings, most of these buildings, which are commercial buildings, things like that, they're all worthless! They have no productivity in fact! In fact, the entire system, which the skyscraper system has in Manhattan, is *worthless*! It doesn't produce any wealth!

### Take Over the Assets

Well, what are we going to do? It's very simple for me, because I have mean streaks in me. I say, "OK, they're bankrupt. All these skyscrapers are bankrupt—not all of them, but most of them are bankrupt. The things that boosted them up there, they're bankrupt! So what are we going to do? Well, you're bankrupt, buddy. You say we owe you? Well, you're not getting anything, unless it's going to be poor relief." You may save them, trying to ship them out someplace where they won't be a tax on the U.S. population.

But all those skyscrapers and all the things with it, the Manhattan skyscrapers, this stuff is *worthless*, essentially worthless in this present form.

Well, what we do is we'll take these properties, and we will rehabilitate these properties to cause them to be under the control of *useful* investments. We don't want Manhattan to go bankrupt! We want the sinners to go bankrupt, and therefore we will take whatever assets

that lie in Manhattan, and we will be able to use them for public purposes. Because we must sustain New York City. And New York City is sick with this thing; it's suffocating with it, and the solution is, we'll shut down Wall Street! *Shut down Wall Street!* Just do it.

How do you do that? The Federal government takes over. And therefore, then you get a new kind of economy working inside Manhattan. Because you can use the buildings. [laughter, applause]

**Q:** Hello, J—V— from the Bronx, I'm here to ask another question. Earlier you said that the education system was complete crap, and that my generation is destructive, and the youth is not going in a very progressive way. And so, I need to bring to your attention the foundation that Lynn Yen has been working on. See, earlier, I told you about the music portion, but I didn't tell you about the science portion that we've been learning with Bill Ferguson, and Chuck and Zeke.

We've been learning about the Kepler solids, and we've also been learning about the doubling of the square, the Socratic method of teaching, and other effective learning styles. But one important thing that Bill has taught us, especially: the reason us human beings aren't like animals, is that we tend to think for the future. And the animals only think for now and their survival, and hope they'll get to the next day. People tend to make bank investments, so that years down the road they can retire with a little bit of wealth, and so they don't have to worry about working any more. So if children are the investment for today, my generation, why aren't we doing more about that? You know?

### Rebuilding after a Century of Decay

**LaRouche:** Very simple: Because we're not providing the kind of mechanisms which are required to achieve that actual goal. Now, you're talking about things, which are attempts to promote those goals. That is not something to be discouraged at all. But nonetheless, the question is, will the education and related improvements considered, will they be sufficient to do the job? Because there's something here, there's an intention, which has to be realized. And it means that you cannot—you mentioned a few things; now these things are not unuseful, but they're not adequate.

And therefore, what you need to do is find an institution which is well-meaning; makes contributions which could be useful in the future, for the development of children and adults and so forth, and that's good! But you have to determine what the standard is that you

*Workers with the Works Progress Administration build a road in Pennsylvania.*

Yes, you're talking about some things are useful, but are they useful enough to save society? Or are they like toys that you can play with to a certain point, and then somebody comes in, and their hand takes the toys away from you—when you thought they were going to be machines. And that's what the danger is.

What kind of an education are these young people going to have, to meet the scientific standard which is required to achieve, what we must achieve; we have to have a standard which meets the standard for the future of mankind, not just the things that will make things better for us temporarily now.

**Q:** Hello, this is Mrs. J—T—. My question is, did General Dempsey resign from Joint Chiefs of Staff voluntarily? And my second question is, did General Allen and General Breedlove et al. attempt a coup d'état over Obama recently?

**LaRouche:** I didn't quite understand. Give it more explanation. [repeats the question]

Oh sure! Oh yes, I know of that, of course. That's a very serious threat. And it's a tough one we're going to have to deal with. You're talking about Breedlove;

**Q:** [follow-up] Yes, did either Allen or Breedlove attempt a coup d'état, recently? Or anyone else?

### Shut Down Obama

**LaRouche:** There are attempts to do exactly that. No question! That requires, really, an awareness among the citizens to realize that that exists! If the citizens will not respond to those threats, then the citizens will find themselves—where? In slavery or worse. And the problem is the gutlessness of people, especially in positions of power, who refuse to protect the people against such machinations. You got a bunch of gutless wonders out there, among the members of Congress.

But my job is, and my intention is to shake things up sufficiently that we can probably get some leverage to do something about that. And I'm doing this on an international scale; I'm involved in things internationally. We must *shut down Obama!* If we don't shut down Obama, you haven't got a chance; the case is hopeless

have to meet, to bring that population up to the level of skills, so that they really have authority. And therefore, the question is the adequacy of the effort we're putting in, trying to take people from the streets, so to speak, and trying to develop them to the point where they have an *independent* ability at skills.

So a few skills, yes, that's good. It's not to be opposed at all, but we know that there's a higher objective which is required to give people the degree of skills, by modern standards, which will enable the people employed to reach levels of achievement way beyond what they're trying to do on a scale today. So therefore, we need a bigger system to make sure that we take what we're doing now, as you've described some of these things. You want to do those things—yes! But they are only preliminary steps. And you want to accelerate that skill, and you need additional means to make sure that your supplying that rate of acceleration of skills, so that by the time some young person gets to the point of adulthood, they really have adult scientific capabilities, or whatever scientific thing they're doing.

But you need a population whose scientific skills meet the standard, which we have failed to meet since the beginning of the Twentieth Century. So therefore, we have almost a whole century to rebuild. And therefore, we have to base ourselves on understanding where we have to go, where we have to go and how we have to go, to meet the requirements for mankind now.

CC/Urban

*One of Manhattan's most useless towers, the Trump Tower, seen from 5th Avenue, 2005.*

unless you shut down Obama. Unless you put everything you've got into getting rid of Obama; you don't have a chance unless you do that.

**Q:** Mr. LaRouche, my name is J— and my question is, how do you see the stock market activities that have been happening over this last week, and the trans-Atlantic system as the driver of war?

**LaRouche:** I'm glad you asked that! You may like my answer; or you may be frightened by it, one of the two!

No, look, Wall Street is hopelessly bankrupt. Wall Street is hopelessly bankrupt! Right now, we're on the edge of a folding-up of Wall Street. That is one of the spurs which is impelling people to do what they're doing, in desperation, because they don't want to accept the fact that Wall Street is absolutely worthless; it's much less than worthless. And Wall Street has to disappear!

And as I indicated earlier, in an earlier remark, what we want to do is take Manhattan's Wall Street area and adjacent areas; we take that over. Why do we take it

over, and how do we take it over? Well, Manhattan has a right to intervene, in saying they've got to protect the rights of Manhattan. Now what that means is, that Manhattan will take over all the bankrupt system of the Wall Street systems. It'll just shoo 'em out!

What we're going to have to do, is take those properties, skyscrapers and so forth on Wall Street, we're going to have find some way to use these things for an economically beneficial purpose, and we're going to kick all the people out of their little towers, and we're going change the function of those towers, as best we can, to get some use out of them. We're probably going to have free lunches, or as they say, free rent or cheap rent, in the Wall Street area.

## Foreclose Manhattan

We're going to have to do that, because we're going to have to generate a source of income to maintain Manhattan, at the time that Manhattan otherwise is going bankrupt. We have to foreclose on Manhattan! And we will do similar things in other parts of the United States where it's appropriate.

But we have to understand, Wall Street *is dead*! And if you don't recognize that, you're going to be next on the dead list, so therefore, you've got to take action in order to save your own economy.

Like the Manhattan economy, how are you going to save it? Wall Street's not going to pay the rents any more! Because Wall Street's bankrupt, and it can't pay the rents. So aren't we going to take these properties that Wall Street cannot afford to maintain; and aren't we going to use some of these properties as much as we can, to create a new kind of rental system, of building up operations which are going to be useful, in Manhattan? We're going to take properties which Wall Street cannot cover any more, and we're going to take 'em over, put 'em through reorganization. And if necessary, we'll charge rentals to these territories. And when we use those rentals which we gave, we are now the landlords; Manhattan is now the landlord: When a Wall Street bank goes broke, then Manhattan takes over the property of that Wall Street bank.

So, in that case, you've got a new system. But this kind of thing has been done before, but the fact of the matter is that Wall Street is absolutely worthless. It's less than worthless.

And right now, as we speak, sit and speak here right now, the breakdown point, the absolute collapse of Wall Street, is in the air. But the moment that it's going to

**But we have to understand, Wall Street is dead! And if you don't recognize that, you're going to be next on the dead list, so therefore, you've got to take action in order to save your own economy.**

**Like the Manhattan economy, how are you going to save it? Wall Street's not going to pay the rents any more! Because Wall Street's bankrupt, and it can't pay the rents. So aren't we going to take these properties that Wall Street cannot afford to maintain; and aren't we going to use some of these properties as much as we can, to create a new kind of rental system, of building up operations which are going to be useful, in Manhattan? We're going to take properties which Wall Street cannot cover any more, and we're going to take 'em over, put 'em through reorganization. And if necessary, we'll charge rentals to these territories. And when we use those rentals which we get, we are now the landlords; Manhattan is now the landlord: When a Wall Street bank goes broke, then Manhattan takes over the property of that Wall Street bank.**

occur is not certain. But the occurrence is inevitable. [applause]

**Q:** This is H— from the Bronx, and I've been thinking about this world war process and the history of this. It's interesting, before World War I the Italians attacked Libya, and they were attacking the Ottoman Empire, and that led into the Serbs attacking the Ottoman Empire, and the Archduke being assassinated later in Austria, and you know what happened next, right?

And we had World War II not too much after that. First, we had Fascism in Italy, and then the Nazis in Germany, and the Civil War in Spain which sort of put everything together for what followed.

And since 2011, we've again had an attack on Libya; we had the Arab Spring process which sort of led into ISIS; and then we had parallel to this, the Ukrainian Nazis' rise, and behind that, you have interesting things possibly from the Arab-Israeli sector. So how can we control this process of radical nationalism, which seems to be the trigger for a war, either very soon or after?

### For the Nation and Civilization

**LaRouche:** Well, the occurrence of such a war, the war you sort of point out, is not something which mankind can easily survive. We're on the edge of a system which—we could actually have a virtual extinction of the human species, and it could occur in very short period of time right now. We don't wish that to happen, but it can happen, and it's ready to happen. If Obama remains the President of the United States, that will

happen! That will be the effect.

Now, we have forces, however, in the planet Earth which are not willing to accept that. But the problem is, how do we organize the change of behavior, so that we bring positive forces into play rather than the devilish ones. And that's what the problem is.

I mean, this is something which, for me, is a living process; it's not something that I'm speculating on, or what to talk about as such. This is what I live on: That I have a mission here to contribute to getting mankind out of this mess, and I have some skills at this, which, despite my age and infirmities and whatnot, that's what has to be done; that's what I do. I'm committed to this, and I'm very deeply committed to Manhattan. And I have been.

I have had a project of saying, we've got to do something about Manhattan, ever since some time ago; October of last year, I made a decision, I was going to move in on Manhattan, because Manhattan was going to be the most useful vehicle for organizing the United States itself. And there's a real basis for that: Alexander Hamilton, if he were alive today, would explain that to you, what Manhattan is all about. And that's what I'm fighting for.

I'm fighting for the whole nation, I'm fighting for civilization, and I know that my mission is to take a vocal point, on responsibility for trying to protect Manhattan, because of what Manhattan represents to Alexander Hamilton, for example, and to me, even though I haven't been in Manhattan for a very long time, by default of old age. I would have been here more often,

*Alexander Hamilton's gravesite, located in the yard of Trinity Church in lower Manhattan, is only a stone's throw from Wall Street.*

except I was getting old.

## The Mission of the USA

But that's what I'm committed to: I'm committed to a mission, and the mission includes the emphasis on the importance of Manhattan for the United States, because Manhattan's not just a place, it's a center; it always has been, ever since Alexander Hamilton came into town. And therefore, Manhattan must be ensured, to live on, to fulfill its mission as was intended implicitly by Alexander Hamilton. And Hamilton's understanding of New York City was the correct understanding of the intention of the existence of the United States itself, and that is true right now.

**Q:** Good afternoon, I have three questions: What kind of quality does a President need? You say mathematics is not a science; how can you prove science without mathematics?

**LaRouche:** Mathematics is not very important. It's not that important. Mathematics was a mistake. What happened is, we have a progress of physical science, up through the period of the Nineteenth Century, and the last decade of the Nineteenth Century was a change-over pause, where you had some great scientists, who were leaders at that point, which include Einstein, for example, who was one of the greatest of these leaders. And what we were doing then, was founding, attempting to found, a great system of physical economy.

The United States had already been an organizing center for physical economy. this had happened under Abraham Lincoln, for example; it happened under a great President who served after Lincoln's death, and on others. So those motives, which are motives which spring from Alexander Hamilton's intention for the Americas, these are the things which are the most precious, because they are things which have to be understood by the people of the United States, who can grasp what these things actually mean, what these principles are; what they mean, and what they mean for future generations. Because when you're talking about human beings, you're not talking about *a* generation, you're talking about a succession of generations. Because human beings are permanent fixtures; that is, they may die, but the meaning of their life lives on.

And it's that attitude about mankind, which is the attitude which is exemplified by Alexander Hamilton. what he was doing. And you can say, you can go down to the Southern part of Manhattan, and you can see a residence where he is buried. And every time you see that place, and you see the marks of Wall Street there, you have a certain shuddering feeling about the whole matter.

But Alexander Hamilton represented the very soul of the development and creation of not only Manhattan, but of the United States itself. And so therefore, our responsibility is to recognize that we all are going to die, as I will die in due course, I suppose, sooner or later; and what's important, is what we represent in creating some progress for mankind in general. And we think of this not just in terms of Manhattan; we think of it in terms of the United States generally, despite the Southern regions of the United States, which appall me. But these are things which we must give our dedication to, even within the proximity of the limitation of our own lives. And it's when we are participating in creating an improved future that we justify our own existence. And we have to look at things that way.

**Q:** [follow-up] Third question: I see the mathematics everywhere. When you come out of your house, you can see the mathematics; you go into the road, you go to school, everywhere, there's mathematics everywhere. You count money, this is mathematics; when you drive the car, you see mathematics; how many avenues, how many roads, everything uses mathematics. How can you live without mathematics?

Mathematics uses our whole life. We cannot go without mathematics.

**LaRouche:** I can assure you that's not the case. [laughter] Because mathematics is a corrupt method. There are other methods of physical science which are superior, but the use of mathematics, the standards of mathematics as being science, is a swindle. So don't depend upon mathematics; depend upon science, *not* mathematics.

**LaRouche:** [Concludes.] OK! It's not difficult for me. No, the point is that,—I'll put it this way: My particular qualifications are deeply rooted, in family background and so forth, ancestors, and so forth, so I've always been an independent person. I have never submitted, willingly, to anything I didn't believe in. And I still do that.

Now, the result is that I'm very critical of what are considered popular subjects, including allegedly popular scientific subjects. And I am absolutely merciless in dealing with those kinds of things, not because I'm malicious, but because I know that people should not be swallowing that kind of filth; essentially; and that we need a system of education of a type which guarantees that more people will be educated, really educated, and not given arithmetic as a replacement and substitute for science; most of the stuff that's called science today is not science; it's mathematics. And mathematics is *not* science. It never was.

I was trained in the school of Bernhard Riemann. And that was my qualified background, and that's what I still represent today. I have my own additions to this process, but that's what it was all about. And I know that most of what's called science and so forth, contains a great deal of nonsense.

But what I love, is the question of the free spirit, that actually gives up and does not try to copy what somebody else has said, this is the popular thing to believe; but those who really zealously seek out and accomplish the real principles of science, the true principles of science. Not the second-hand variety, called mathematics.

# Every Day Counts In Today's Showdown To Save Civilization

That's why you need *EIR*'s **Daily Alert Service**, a strategic overview compiled with the input of Lyndon LaRouche, and delivered to your email 5 days a week.

For example: On July 27 Lyndon LaRouche identified this August as a period of maximum danger that President Barack Obama will launch provocations against Russia that could lead to the thermonuclear extinction of mankind.

EIR's July 28 Alert featured LaRouche's evaluation, along with critical intelligence on the Russian strategic doctrine. Throughout the rest of the week, the Alert has pointed to the way Hillary Clinton's exposure of Obama could interrupt Obama's war drive—as well as updates on the worsening threat.

This is intelligence you need to act on, if we are going to survive as a nation and a species. Can you really afford to be without it?

# Do You Have the Guts To Face the Truth and Act in Time?

by Jeffrey Steinberg

Aug 23—The entire global strategic situation can be summed up in two essential facts. First, Wall Street is disintegrating and the entire U.S. economy is about to vanish, unless immediate action is taken. Second, President Barack Obama is moving in the direction of launching thermonuclear war against Russia. He is seeking an element of surprise, trying to outguess the Russians.

The disintegration of Wall Street, already underway, is the driver for Obama's insane planned provocations against Russia. Virtually everything that is presented as news is a diversion, aimed at blinding the American people and world leaders to the simple reality that we are already in an immediate trajectory towards financial and economic disintegration, and a global war of annihilation.

Lyndon LaRouche, in dialogue with a Manhattan audience and close colleagues over the weekend, spelled out the clear solution to this crisis.

First, President Obama must be removed from office, immediately, using provisions of the Twenty-fifth Amendment to the U.S. Constitution, which provides for the removal of a President who is mentally or physically unfit to continue to serve. By virtue of his commitment to provoke thermonuclear war with Russia, Obama has proven that he is insane and unfit to continue.

Former Secretary of State Hillary Clinton can facilitate this process by publicly presenting what she knows about President Obama's willful and lying cover-up of the murders of Ambassador Christopher Stevens and three other American officials in Benghazi, Libya, on

Franklin D. Roosevelt President Library & Museum

*This is the cover graphic of a Special Exhibit on FDR's first hundred days in office.*

Sept. 11, 2012. Up until now, Clinton has been intimidated into silence, just as she was intimidated into initially going along with Obama's lies on the night of the Benghazi 9/11 attack. Now, she must speak the truth to the American people.

There is no way Wall Street can survive. It is already dead. There is, however, a solution. Shut down Wall Street, cut off the flow of any further bailout to Wall Street. Put the current system through bankruptcy reorganization under a restored Glass-Steagall system. Then begin the immediate emission of Federal credit to create jobs, under an economic reconstruction program, modeled on the precise measures adopted by President Franklin D. Roosevelt from the moment he was sworn in as President in March 1933.

Take the Wall Street skyscrapers and convert them into machines of progress, FDR-style.

As LaRouche stated it:

Cancel Wall Street. Put people to work like FDR did. We can get out of this crisis—not without pain, but we can survive and prosper. Listen to the voice of FDR from afar. We must get the American people to stop being stupid and accepting the existing system, as if there was no viable alternative. There is a viable alternative, and it starts by cancelling Wall Street altogether.

Cancel the Obama Presidency and cancel Wall Street, and all of the pressing problems, which are centered exclusively in the trans-Atlantic region, can be solved.

tions known today by the code-word "color revolutions."

In late January 1945, Furtwängler fled Germany to go into exile in Switzerland. While many Jewish musicians had left Germany after Hitler's coup in 1933, Furtwängler had defended Jewish musicians, threatening the Nazis that he would quit conducting if Jewish participants in the Berlin Philharmonic were sent to concentration camps. When Hitler banned performances of the Jewish-born composer Felix Mendelssohn in 1934, Furtwängler conducted that composer's "Midsummer Night's Dream" at a February concert that coincided with a raucous Nazi parade occurring within earshot of the auditorium. The concert audience rose in impassioned and tearful cheers at the close of the music, allying with the defiance shown by Furtwängler, while the Mayor of Leipzig, Carl Friedrich Goerdeler, refused to obey the Nazis' order to tear down the statue of Mendelssohn which since 1892 had stood outside the Gewandhaus concert hall. An enraged Heinrich Himmler, head of the Nazi SS, complained bitterly in a note that "There is no Jew, filthy as he may be, for whom Furtwängler does not stretch out a helping hand."

Goerdeler (whom the Nazis executed on Feb. 2, 1945), was a leading representative of the anti-Hitler Resistance, which also encompassed leading figures of the German military. By the late 1930s, Britain had situated one of its chief moles within U.S. Intelligence to monitor the German anti-Hitler Resistance movement. Allen Dulles, embodiment of a pro-British financier network opposing Gen. William Donovan in America's Office of Strategic Studies (OSS), had moved to Switzerland in order, among other things, to gather information on Europe's anti-fascist movements. In desperation, the German Resistance fell into the trap of relaying all of their attempts to remove Hitler, to Dulles or other British-linked channels. Not surprisingly, every attempt to topple Hitler failed, because the British maintained a policy of *both* supporting Hitler, and of insisting "there is no such thing as good Germans."

Dulles's postwar description of the German Resis-

German Federal Archives

*Carl Friedrich Goerdeler, the Mayor of Leipzig (1933-35), who, like Furtwängler, refused to obey Nazi orders to trash composer Felix Mendelssohn.*

tance, and other sources, such as the chronicles now available on the life of the Germany's famous Pastor Dietrich Bonhoeffer, make clear that music was an indispensable ingredient in sustaining the morale and fight of the anti-Hitler resistance. Many of the leading members of the German resistance were musicians, and Furtwängler's concerts in the capital city of Berlin were among the most important gathering places for Hitler's opponents to congregate. As the prominent German actor Boleslav Barlog later testified at the December 1946 trial against Furtwängler for alleged Nazi collaboration, "For the duration of the Third Reich, Furtwängler was one of the reasons why it was worth staying alive.... If we could have [a concert by Furtwängler], there was no need to despair utterly."

Even though this was well-known to the British elements within the postwar "Denazification" process of determining who was "clean enough" to hold a position of influence in postwar Germany, the Allies moved to isolate Furtwängler and prevent him from returning to the conductor's podium after the war. A picture taken at the one birthday event for Hitler at which Furtwängler was compelled to perform, showing a swastika in the background and Hitler shaking his hand, was used to argue that Furtwängler had been a willing "music-master" for the tyrant.

The truth is that Furtwängler personally ordered that no Nazi symbols be displayed at any rehearsal or concert he participated in. He never accepted any governmental position in the Nazi regime, although the cabinet repeatedly attempted to co-opt him; and by 1936, his secretary was forced to emigrate under threats of imprisonment, putting Furtwängler in a dangerous isolation for much of the regime's existence. With only three exceptions under duress, he kept to his stalwart position that he would never conduct a concert in a country occupied against its will by the Nazis, even though his orchestra was sent there by the Nazi regime under the direction of more compliant conductors.

After a brief retreat in Egypt in 1936, to gather his

thoughts and physically restore his stamina, he remained in Germany to defend the universal culture which he had been surrounded by in his youth, through his father, a famous archeologist.

In December 1944, friends warned Furtwängler that Hitler, sitting in his madhouse bunker in Berlin, had put him on a list of people to be assassinated. Soon before his departure from Germany, a recording was made of a concer which included Beethoven's "Eroica" Symphony No. 3. With a tension beyond description audible in that recording, the second movement's slow "Funeral March" captures the pending doom of the Nazi regime, which Furtwängler had yearned as early as 1933, would be brought to an end by intervention.

## The Postwar Fraud

It was not until May 1947 that Furtwängler was allowed to re-enter Germany from Switzerland, and to resume his work as the world's most accomplished conductor. Precisely the same London-centered circles who had financed and protected Hitler and his gangster apparatus, now lied that Furtwängler had "supported" Hitler and had used music to strengthen his war effort. This pernicious British role was underlined by the opposite treatment the Allied "Denazification" campaign offered to Furtwängler's long-term rival, the former bandleader Herbert von Karajan, who, during the Hitler dictatorship had been a favorite protégé of Hermann Goering.

Musicians from around the world mobilized to have Furtwängler reinstated in Germany's political life, including prominently the Jewish violinist Yehudi Menuhin. Menuhin sent a wire in February 1946 to U.S. Gen. John McClure, who had just issued an official ban forbidding Furtwängler from conducting anywhere in the Western Occupied Zones:

> ... I do not believe that the fact of remaining in one's own country, particularly when fulfilling a job of this nature akin to a spiritual Red Cross or minister's mission, is alone sufficient enough to condemn a man. On the contrary, as a military man you would know that remaining at one's post often requires greater courage than running away. He saved, and for that we are deeply his debtors, the best part and only salvageable part of his own German culture. As for ... lending 'an aura of respectability to the party' ... are we the Allies not infinitely more guilty, and of our own free will, by recognizing and [making pacts] with

*Violinist Yehudi Menuhin (right) at a studio recording session with Wilhelm Furtwängler in May of 1952. The Jewish Menuhin vigorously defended Furtwängler when he came under attack after World War II.*

these monsters until the last minute, when almost despite ourselves, we were literally dragged and unchivalrously knocked into the struggle?...

While London's efforts to try to break Furtwängler's identity and get him to retire failed, through insidious maneuvers, a degenerated club of unqualified frauds were increasingly promoted to dominate the musical environment, not only in Germany, but throughout the world.

In one instance, only one month after the Allies liberated Berlin, Leo Borchard, an anti-fascist resistance fighter who also happened to be a conductor, launched a campaign to immediately resume the Berlin Philharmonic, hoping that Furtwängler would soon return. He organized concerts in bombed-out buildings and conducted them himself as a placeholder. One evening in Berlin, in August 1945, as he was being chauffeured home by a British colonel following a dinner party, Borchard was shot dead by an American sentry, after the colonel, who was the driver, failed to acknowledge the sentry's flashlight signals. Fortunately, a Romanian immigrant student named Sergiu Celibidache, likewise an ardent admirer of Furtwängler, who had survived in Berlin on a student visa, picked up the baton, and continued the revival of Berlin's famous orchestra.

Less overt than this incident, the British cultural offensive also included drawing the United States into the wild preparations for what became in 1950 the Congress for Cultural Freedom, a propaganda zoo whose purpose was to use the excuse of fighting Communism to crush all "idealistic" philosophies. An early publication which set the stage for the Allen Dulles-supported CCF was the publication of a bizarre book focussed on music by the "popular" intellectual author Thomas Mann. A fictional fantasy reflecting the explicitly anti-Furtwängler views of such ideologues as Theodor Adorno and the atonal composer Arnold Schoenberg, the novel was titled *Dr. Faustus* in honor of the medieval tale of what happens to those who make a pact with the Devil. In the book, it is explicitly argued that the great composer Ludwig von Beethoven was a demonic personality, and that the only way for genius to be exercised in music, is through the acquisition of a Faustian worldview of admiring evil.

Thus was announced through this kind of British-sponsored propaganda, the brainwashing outlook of a twisted logic that asserts that those who claim to help mankind by developing the human mind are deluded victims of a pathological love of evil; and that those who despise genius are the only ones qualified to lead society.

## Genius Touches Genius

Lyndon LaRouche's first encounter with Furtwängler was in 1946, when the 22-year-old, while stationed in India, heard Furtwängler's 1938 recording of Tchaikovsky's "Pathétique" Symphony No. 6 with the Berlin Philharmonic. The power of Furtwängler's genius hit him like a thunderclap, shaping his future development as a physical economist, philosopher, Presidental candidate, and statesman.

Among the many occasions when LaRouche has referred to this formative time of his life, is the following footnote from his Jan. 23, 2000 article "The Issue of Mind-Set," which he wrote in commemoration of the 80th birthday of his close friend Prof. Grigori L. Bondarevsky, a member of the Russian Academy of Social Sciences:

In Classical composition, and in its performance, there is no dissonance as such. Rather, there are transitions integral to a process of ongoing development. For such purposes, the formal dissonance must be performed as precisely such a transition, by emphasizing both the harmonic and metrical transitions themselves as the defining, developmental actions within the composition as an integral entirety. This is the action which lies 'between the notes,' which must never be used as arbitrary dissonance, as in Romantic chromaticism, as in so-called 'passage work.' Thus, in Classical performance, the way in which the conductor or performing artist attacks the composition, as from a moment before the start, is decisive in putting across the composer's intent.

I, for one, first recognized this as a distinct and lawful principle, during early 1946, in a U.S. Army replacement depot outside Calcutta, India, at first hearing of Furtwängler's conducting of a Tchaikovsky symphony, in an HMV recording. The same principle is characteristic of the required performance of all works in a strophic form, in Classical poetry or music: there must be a progressive variation in enunciation among the strophes, a variation which, taken over the breath of the composition, from beginning to close, is metaphorical in character, which prompts the performance to move the audience's mind in the way corresponding to the intended metaphor which the composer has defined by the closing of the composition as an integrated whole.

That 1938 recording is widely available today, and one cannot fail to be impressed by how different it is from virtually every other conductor's recording of this work. Whereas most conductors seek whatever sonic effects are necessary to evoke an mindless "emotional state"—which is the hallmark of the Romantic mindset—Furtwängler takes Tchaikovsky's *musical ideas* more seriously than perhaps even the composer himself, reshaping the symphony with ironical juxtapositions that lift the listener out of the muck of "sincere feelings," and into the truly human, Classical realm of the Sublime.

Nowhere is this touch of genius more evident than in Furtwängler's post-war recordings of Franz Schubert's Sympony No. 9, which occupied La-Rouche's intense attention during the early 1950s when, now in his thirties, he was making his history-making discoveries in the science of physical economy. Indeed, uniquely in Furtwängler's mind-set, LaRouche saw mankind's real future, his true destiny. As he remarked during a discussion on Aug. 13, 2015:

> And therefore, what you're singing, you're singing in terms as Furtwängler would perform it, as he did with his treatment of the Schubert *Ninth Symphony*, which is a relevant point of reference; is that it forces you to recognize, that you can reach something, which is the future of mankind. That means that you are able to come up with ideas, which go beyond anything that mankind had previously imagined. And instead of trying to build, mechanically, by mechanical pieces, like jigsaw puzzle pieces, we actually are creating a higher form of human experience, in the

universe and otherwise. This is the thing that distinguishes mankind from the animals. And unfortunately, many musicians are actually under those terms, animals, practicing as animals.

It's the meaning of performing music, *between* the notes, which defines a reflection of the difference of man from beast.

Although Furtwängler was not an economist, he would have been the first to acknowledge Lyndon La-Rouche's concept that physical economy and Classical culture are not separate departments, but are essential facets of a truly human mind-set. In the 2004 pamphlet *Children of Satan III*, LaRouche wrote:

> The most essential consideration, therefore, is the need to promote the development of those mental powers of the individual which generate revolutionary changes in practice to the effect of increasing the net physical productivity of society per capita and per square kilometer.

Only what meets that criterion, can be properly judged as truthful.

# Abraham Lincoln & John Quincy Adams: Acting Against Evil

by Robert Ingraham

August 23—*Shall evil be allowed to rule over our nation? Shall the Constitutional Office of the Presidency be so far perverted that it no longer bears any resemblance to its original intent? Shall a monstrosity inhabit the White House and drag the nation to its doom?*

Such, clearly, is the challenge we face today, in August of 2015, as Barack Obama lies, blackmails, bullies, kills, and pushes both America and the rest of humanity to the abyss of thermonuclear war. Those with eyes can see this danger. But seeing is merely passive, an existentialist exercise. What is needed are those with courage to *act before it is too late*.

Events in history never truly repeat themselves, and drawing a direct parallel between the crisis of today, a threat of thermonuclear annihilation which has no precedent in human history, and crises of the past is impossible. However, what is possible, what is most certainly relevant, is to examine the qualities of leadership demonstrated by courageous individuals from our history—

Library of Congress

*The War Crisis of 1846-48: The Mexican-American War, here depicted in a lithograph by John Cameron with the aid of Nathaniel Currier.*

leadership born from a willingness to act. Such courage, such actions, have accomplished great things before, and such is what is needed now.

## I. Leadership and Crisis

One such example occurred fourteen years before the outbreak of the United States Civil War. On May 13, 1846, at the request of the slave-owning President James Polk,[1] the United States declared war on the Republic of Mexico. In his war message to Congress, Polk charged that the Mexican Army, "after a long-continued series of menaces, have at last invaded our territory and shed the blood of our fellow-citizens on our own soil." Six months later, in his annual address to Congress, Polk defended the ongoing war by stating that the war was "neither desired nor provoked by the United States;" that Mexico had "commenced hostilities, and... forced war upon us;" and that "Mexico became the aggressor by invading our soil in hostile array and shedding the blood of our citizens on our own soil." In this speech Polk accused opponents of the war of treason, by giving "aid and comfort" to the enemy of the United States.

The truth, much as in today's long-nurtured plans for thermonuclear confrontation by the British Empire against Russia, is that the desired war with Mexico was years in preparation, with the intent, by the Southern Slave Power, to annex huge sections of that nation's territory—some went so far as to propose annexing all of Mexico—to the United States for the avowed purpose of opening vast new areas for the expansion of slavery. At the conclusion of the war, President Polk was known to have favored the proposal

Library of Congress

*John Quincy Adams, dubbed "Old Man Eloquent" for his fight against slavery in his terms as Congressman from Massachusetts (1830-1848).*

by then Senator Jefferson Davis to seize not only California, New Mexico, and Arizona, but the provinces of Tamaulipas, Baja California, Nuevo León, Coahuila, and Chihuahua as well.

If the war had proceeded without opposition, and if the plans of the Slave Power had been entirely successful, then the years leading up to 1860 would have been far different in character, and the ensuing history of the United States radically altered. But courage and leadership intervened.

## II. Enter John Quincy Adams

John Quincy Adams entered the U.S. House of Representatives in 1831 and would serve there for seventeen years. During those years, Adams devoted all of his energies to one single heroic task—battling, often alone, against the ascendent Slave Power of the Southern states.[2] This included his eight-year fight against the "Gag Rule" in the House of Representatives which prohibited any discussion of slavery on the floor of the House, as well as his successful 1841 argument before the U.S. Supreme Court in the Amistad Case.

Polk's war message to Congress was delivered on May 11, 1846. Initially, there was widespread opposition in Congress to a Declaration of War, but with Congressmen facing the likelihood of being labeled unpatriotic or even traitors, over the next forty-eight hours resistance to the war drive crumbled, and when the vote for war was taken on May 13th, there were 174 ayes against only 14 nays. At the top of the list of "no" votes was John Quincy Adams.

The Mexican-American war lasted twenty-one

---

1. James K. Polk of North Carolina, was the last of eight U.S. Presidents to own slaves while in the White House. Andrew Jackson was another, and the remaining six were all from Virginia.

2. Shortly before his death, Adams would write of his seventeen-year battle against the Slave Power in the House of Representatives, that he considered it the only truly great accomplishment of his life. For more on his battles, see Henderson, Denise M., "John Quincy Adams' Battles for the American System," *EIR*, Nov. 16. 2007.

months. For that entire period it was Quincy Adams who led the opposition, and who was the most courageous in speaking "truth to evil." Others joined him or acted on their own, but it was Adams, on the floor of Congress, who took the point. On May 25, 1846, Adams delivered a speech to the House of Representatives proclaiming that the War was a prearranged plot to extend slavery, and charging that the sending of U.S. troops to Mexico was a "southern expedition to find bigger pens to cram with slaves."

At every step of the war, Adams fought to limit the fighting and end the conflict, continually recruiting a steady stream of new allies in the House to the anti-war fight. This had the effect of ending the war much earlier than the Polk administration desired, and limiting the amount of territory seized. Adams also spearheaded the successful effort for passage of the Wilmot Proviso by the House, which would have prohibited the introduction of slavery into any new territory gained from Mexico. Despite his strenuous efforts, the Proviso was defeated in the Senate.

It was also during this period, that for two years, from 1847 to 1849, Adams took under his wing the freshman Congressman from Illinois, Abraham Lincoln.

Library of Congress
*President James K. Polk (1845-1849)*

## III. Enter Abraham Lincoln

Abraham Lincoln was morally opposed to slavery from a very early age. One incident from his young adulthood demonstrates the depth of his feeling on the subject. After a river trip, with friends and associates to New Orleans, once arrived, he and his companions happened upon a slave auction in progress, and, according to eyewitness accounts, Lincoln was so overcome with horror and moral revulsion that he was reduced to tears and couldn't speak.

Yet, Lincoln's early political career was a different matter. Passionately committed to policies of economic development, he rarely publicly spoke of slav-

ery, and it is clear that, for the pre-1846 Lincoln, slavery was primarily a personal and moral matter, not a political issue. The Mexican-American War and his two years in Congress changed all that.

Part of Lincoln's transformation began earlier in Illinois, a state originally settled by (mostly) slave-owners from Kentucky and Virginia. Even in Lincoln's time *de facto* slavery (Black Codes) existed in Illinois, particularly in the southern Little Cairo section of the state. However, between 1825 and 1846, thousands of Northerners had emigrated to Illinois via the Erie Canal route, primarily from New York and New England, dramatically changing the culture and political make-up of the state. By the time of Lincoln's election to Congress, these Northerners comprised a majority of the state's population.

As early as 1837, Lincoln had submitted a protest in the Illinois House against that state's Black Codes, and between 1844 and 1846 Lincoln began to develop deeper ties and relationships to members of the Free Soil movement and the Liberty Party[3] in Illinois. By the time he left for Washington, D.C., Lincoln's recognition of slavery as a *political threat* to the nation had clearly begun to emerge.

### The Spot Resolutions

On December 7, 1847, President Polk delivered his third annual message to Congress. Once again, he championed the war and accused Mexico of "invading the territory of the United States, striking the first blow, and shedding the blood of our citizens on our own soil." Lincoln was in attendance.

Fifteen days later, on December 22nd, after only slightly more than two weeks in office, the freshman Lincoln stood to deliver a speech which historians have dubbed the "Spot Resolutions." In a display of the type of courage sorely needed today, Lincoln directly challenged the veracity of President Polk, while simultane-

---

3. An abolitionist national political party.

ously attacking the legal basis for the war itself.

Polk had claimed that the Mexican Army had invaded the United States and "shed the blood of our fellow-citizens on our own soil." Lincoln demanded: *Show me the spot* where this occurred. He asked:[4]

*First*: Whether the spot of soil on which the blood of our citizens was shed, as in his messages declared, was, or was not, within the territories of Spain, at least from the treaty of 1819 until the Mexican revolution.

*Second*: Whether that spot is, or is not, within the territory which was wrested from Spain, by the Mexican revolution.

*Third*: Whether that spot is, or is not, within a settlement of people, which settlement had existed ever since long before the Texas revolution, until its inhabitants fled from the approach of the U.S. Army.

*Fifth*: Whether the People of that settlement... had ever, previous to the bloodshed, mentioned in his messages, submitted themselves to the government or laws of Texas, or of the United States...

*Sixth*: Whether the People of that settlement, did, or did not, flee from the approach of the United States Army, leaving unprotected their homes and their growing crops, before the blood was shed, as in his messages stated. . . .

*Eighth*: Whether the military force of the United States... was, or was not, so sent into that settlement, after General Taylor had, more than once, intimated to the War Department that, in his opinion, no such movement was necessary to the defense or protection of Texas.

Library of Congress

*Abraham Lincoln as a member of the U.S. House of Representatives, 1847-1849. The photo was taken by one of his law students.*

The "Spot" in question was a small village named Rancho de Carricitos, just north of the Rio Grande in Mexican territory, where on April 25, 1846 American and Mexican troops engaged in an armed conflict. The immediate spark to the conflict was the response of Mexican forces to an invasion by the United States of Mexican sovereign soil.

In order to comprehend the genius and significance of Lincoln's intervention, some background on earlier events, as well the actual motives of the Polk Administration, are required here.

In 1845, the United States annexed the Republic of Texas. During its short-lived period of independence, Texas had claimed the Rio Grande as its southern border, but no one else, including both the Mexican and the United States governments, recognized that claim. Historically, the pre-1836 Mexican Province of Texas ended at the Nueces River, about 150 miles north of the Rio Grande, and during the entirety of the existence of the Texas Republic, Mexico claimed this as the boundary, and Texas never stationed troops, collected taxes, established courts, or delivered mail south of the Nueces River. Almost all of the residents of the thinly populated region between the Nueces and Rio Grande were Mexicans, living under Mexican jurisdiction.

In July of 1845, Polk ordered 3,500 American troops to enter Texas and take up positions along the Nueces River. Three months later he ordered them to cross the Nueces and proceed to the Rio Grande. This move into Mexican territory was done by Presidential order, with no Congressional approval. In November of 1845, with U.S. troops occupying the "Nueces Strip," Polk deployed John Slidell to Mexico to offer the Mexican government $25 million for Mexico's recognition of the Rio Grande boundary, as well as for the purchase of

---

4. What follows are excerpts from the Resolutions.

California and New Mexico.[5] When, by early 1846, Mexico had made clear that they would not cede or sell any territory, the next step for the Slave Power was to provoke a war.

On April 23, 1846 Mexico announced its readiness to fight a "defensive war" to protect Mexican territory. Two days later 2,000 Mexican calvary crossed the Rio Grande to defend Mexican territory, culminating in the clash at Rancho de Carricitos, the "Spot" where American (and Mexican) blood was spilt.

## The Power of Speaking the Truth

Beginning with his first War Message to Congress on May 11, 1846, and continuing through to December 1847, President Polk had repeated in almost every public address, official statement, and message to Congress, that the war with Mexico was justified to repel Mexican aggression and to avenge the spilling of American blood on American soil. After Lincoln's Spot Resolutions speech, he never again made that argument.

Lincoln had both demolished the legal justification for the war itself, and exposed the President as willfully lying to both the Congress and the American people. Representatives of the Slave Power in the House of Representatives prevented Lincoln's Resolutions from coming to a vote, but neither President Polk nor anyone else from among the Southern war party tried to answer Lincoln's charges—because they could not answer them.

Twelve days after Lincoln's Spot Resolutions, on January 3, 1848, the House of Representatives voted 85 to 81 to censure the President, passing a resolution (sponsored by George Ashmun from Massachusetts) which stated that the Mexican War had been "unneces-

*George Ashmun, a Whig member of the House of Representatives from Massachusetts (1845-1851), who crafted the successful resolution of censure against President Polk.*

sarily and unconstitutionally" begun.[6] Lincoln and Quincy Adams both voted for the Censure. The House directed that a committee of five Senators and five Representatives meet with President Polk "to advise and consult upon the best mode of terminating the existing war with Mexico in a manner honorable and just to both belligerents."

Nine days later, on January 12th, Lincoln spoke again on the House floor, elaborating the legal validity of the charges contained in his Spot Resolutions, and driving home the point that the President had consistently lied for eighteen months as to the origin and justification for the war. Additionally, Lincoln then proceeded to question the actual war aims of the Administration. An excerpt from this speech reads:

Let him (Polk) answer, fully, fairly, and candidly. Let him answer with facts, and not with arguments. Let him remember he sits where Washington sat, and so remembering, let him answer, as Washington would answer. As a nation should not, and the Almighty will not, be evaded, so let him attempt no evasion—no equivocation. And if, so answering, he can show that the soil was ours, where the first blood of the war was shed—that it was not within an inhabited country, or, if within such, that the inhabitants had submitted themselves to the civil authority of Texas, or of the United States, then I am with him for his justification. In that case I, shall be most happy to reverse the vote I gave the other day....

But if he can not, or will not do this—if on any pretence, or no pretence, he shall refuse or omit it, then I shall be fully convinced, of what I more than suspect already, that he is deeply conscious of being in the wrong—that he feels the

---

5. Slidell later became a leading figure in the Confederacy who was deployed to London and Paris in an attempt to bring France and England into the Civil War on the side of the South. Polk's instructions to Slidell demonstrate that Polk knew that the Nueces-Rio Grande Strip was actually Mexican territory. They also reveal that, for Polk and the slave interests, the acquisition of Texas was only a stepping-stone, and the seizure of all or parts of Mexico was clearly the plan from the beginning.

6. Ashmun's original language stated that the war had been "unnecessarily and unconstitutionally begun by the President of the United States," which would have represented grounds for impeachment.

blood of this war, like the blood of Abel, is crying to Heaven against him. That originally having some strong motive—what, I will not stop now to give my opinion concerning—to involve the two countries in a war, and trusting to escape scrutiny, by fixing the public gaze upon the exceeding brightness of military glory—that attractive rainbow, that rises in showers of blood—that serpent's eye, that charms to destroy—he plunged into it, and has swept, on and on, till, disappointed in his calculation of the ease with which Mexico might be subdued, he now finds himself, he knows not where. How like the half insane mumbling of a fever-dream, is the whole war part of his late message! At one time telling us that Mexico has nothing whatever, that we can get, but territory; at another, showing us how we can support the war, by levying contributions on Mexico...

Having it now settled that territorial indemnity is the only object, we are urged to seize, by legislation here, all that he was content to take, a few months ago, and the whole province of lower California to boot, and to still carry on the war—to take all we are fighting for, and still fight on. Again, the President is resolved, under all circumstances, to have full territorial indemnity for the expenses of the war... he insists that the separate national existence of Mexico, shall be maintained; but he does not tell us how this can be done, after we shall have taken all her territory. Lest the questions, I here suggest, be considered speculative merely, let me be indulged a moment in trying [to] show they are not. The war has gone on some twenty months; for the expenses of which, together with an inconsiderable old score, the President now claims about one half of the Mexican territory; and that, by far the better half....[7]

Several days after delivering this speech, in a letter to his law partner William Herndon, Lincoln was explicit as to the threat to the existence to the nation posed by Polk's actions:

That soil was not ours; and Congress did not annex or attempt to annex it. But to return to

your position: Allow the President to invade a neighboring nation, whenever *he* shall deem it necessary to repel an invasion, and you allow him to do so, *whenever he may choose to say* he deems it necessary for such purpose—and you allow him to make war at pleasure. Study to see if you can fix *any limit* to his power in this respect....

## IV. What Courage Can Accomplish

Already censured by the House of Representatives, and facing potentially far worse consequences, Polk soon brought the war to a conclusion. The Treaty of Guadalupe Hidalgo was signed on February 2, 1848 and ratified by the Senate on March 10th, by a vote of 38 to 14. Including Texas, the Treaty represented a loss of 55 percent of Mexico's 1835 territory to the United States, but a proposed amendment by Jefferson Davis to take even more of Mexico was voted down. A subsequent Senate vote to enforce the anti-slavery provisions of the Wilmot Proviso in all the newly acquired territory was defeated 38 to 15.

The unconstitutional Mexican-American War had been launched as a U.S. war of aggression by the slave interests of the South, and, in one sense, the consequences of that war resulted in a subsequent political domination over the United States by the Slave Power which led directly to the Civil War twelve years later. The relentless post-war expansion of the Slave Power across the United States, including the effects of the 1850 Compromise, the 1854 Kansas-Nebraska Act, and the dissolution of the Whig Party, led directly to crisis of 1860 when the Republic of George Washington and Alexander Hamilton was nearly extinguished.

But!, that is not the whole story. The fight, the courage, the leadership provided by Abraham Lincoln, John Quincy Adams, and their allies during 1846-1848 created new potentials for the nation, new opportunities for final victory, and made possible the reality of the later Lincoln Presidency which saved the nation.

From 1847 on, Lincoln would emerge as a leading national opponent of the Slave Power, and he never looked back. After the conclusion of the war, he used what was left of his brief two-year term in office to escalate the fight against Southern domination. In 1848 there were five separate attempts to revive the provisions of the Wilmot Proviso to halt the spread of slavery

---

7. The full speech is available here.

*What the opponents of the Mexican-American war fought: the spread of slave conditions like this shown in a photo of a cotton field in Texas in the Nineteenth Century.*

into the South and West.[8] Lincoln voted for all of them.

He also joined repeatedly with John Quincy Adams to fight the continuing attempts by the slave interests to "gag" any discussion of slavery in the House. Although the Gag Rule had been repealed in 1844, it was still the uniform practice of Southern representatives to make a motion to table (kill) all individual petitions or bills relating to slavery which came before the House. Lincoln voted several times with Adams against the tabling of such petitions.

On January 10, 1849 Lincoln introduced a bill in the House to completely abolish slavery in Washington, D.C. John Calhoun, although serving in the Senate, used his influence in the House to have the bill tabled. In 1862, as President, Lincoln would sign a law freeing all of the Capital's slaves, stating at that time, "I have never doubted the constitutional authority of Congress to abolish slavery in this District, and I have ever desired to see the national capital freed from the institution in some satisfactory way. Hence there has never been in my mind any question upon the subject. . . ."

When Lincoln arose, on Dec. 22, 1847, to deliver his Spot Resolutions to the House of Representatives, a decisive change, an intervention, was accomplished.

---

8. The most serious of these was a bill by Rep. Harvey Putnam of New York, which was defeated 105 to 93.

The ultimate effects of that intervention were not all recognized in 1847, but for Lincoln, his assumption of the leadership in the fight to defeat the Slave Power would change history forever.

## 1848 to 1860

The real lesson to be learned from the actions of Lincoln, Adams, and others during the Mexican-American War is to understand what can be accomplished if an individual or a group of people simply decides to fight. Don't watch. Don't comment. Stand up and fight.

In 1846, the House of Representaives had voted 174 to 14 to declare war against Mexico. Among those fourteen were:

- **John Quincy Adams**
- **Erastus Culver** (New York)— Culver would continue his fight against the Slave Power. In 1850, he, together with John Jay (the grandson of Washington's Supreme Court Justice), successfully argued *Lemmon v. New York*, a case which forced Virginia slave-owners who were traveling through New York City to surrender their slaves under a writ of habeas corpus. Later, in 1860, Culver was an honored guest at the Cooper Union speech by Abraham Lincoln, and sat next to Lincoln on the dais.
- **Columbo Delano** (Ohio)—later to become Ulysses Grant's Secretary of Interior, and a champion of Grant's "Peace Policy" with the western Indians.
- **George Ashmun** (Massachusetts)—Ashmun would later preside over the 1860 Republican national convention which nominated Lincoln for President.

Fourteen out of one hundred eighty-eight is a small percentage. But those fourteen, together with Lincoln, succeeded in shortening the war, limiting the damage, and defining for the nation both the lies and corruption of President Polk, as well as the true war aims of the Southern slave interests behind the war.

*Far more important,* by standing and fighting in 1847-1848, Lincoln and his allies set into motion a potential for a far-greater victory, one which would come with the realization of a Lincoln Presidency in 1861. That victory would never have materialized, never even been possible, without the stand they took against an unconstitutional war and a mad Presidency, fourteen years earlier.

# How JFK Prevented Thermonuclear Holocaust

by Jeffrey Steinberg

Aug. 25—Faced with the prospect of human extinction in a thermonuclear war between the United States and the Soviet Union, during the 13 days in October 1962 known as the "Cuban Missile Crisis," President John F. Kennedy showed extraordinary courage and left no stone unturned to achieve the desired end: a de-escalation of the crisis and an actual breakthrough in U.S.-Soviet relations, out of the gravest moment of crisis humanity had ever faced.

Long before American U-2 spy planes confirmed, in early October 1962, that the Soviets were installing nuclear-armed missiles in Cuba, just 90 miles away from the continental United States, President Kennedy had established a deeply personal exchange of private communications with Soviet Premier Nikita Khrushchov. That extraordinary private dialogue played a significant role in averting nuclear armageddon.

Through that dialogue, Kennedy and Khrushchov reached a personal understanding that, between them, they held the future survival of humanity in their hands—despite their ideological and political differences, which were vast. Already, at that time, both the United States and the Soviet Union possessed arsenals of thermonuclear weapons and long-range delivery systems that would assure the elimination of life on Earth should a full-scale thermonuclear war commence.

On Oct. 22, 1962, after days of secret deliberations with his closest national security advisors, including the Joint Chiefs of Staff, President Kennedy went on national television to present to the American people the evidence of the presence of Soviet thermonuclear weapons and missiles on Cuban soil. He announced that he was establishing a naval blockade—what he called a "quarantine"—around Cuba, knowing that Soviet ships were en route to the island and were carrying more weapons.

John Fitzgerald Kennedy Library

*President Kennedy and Chairman Khrushchov during their meeting in Vienna, Austria, June 1961.*

Hardline advisors to the President were pressing for even more drastic measures and would argue against any kind of diplomatic solution throughout the thirteen days of the crisis.

President Kennedy demonstrated iron will in deploying the naval quarantine, and he had no intention of backing down on his demand for the Soviet ships to turn around, and for the existing nuclear weapons and missiles to be removed from Cuba. He was, however, committed to pursuing every avenue for war-avoidance.

The day after he delivered his television address, President Kennedy had his personal envoy, Norman Cousins, make direct contact with Pope John XXIII, seeking his assistance in reaching out to Khrushchov for a solution.

On Oct. 24, the Pope sent a personal messsage to Khrushchov, through the Soviet embassy in Rome, imploring him: "The cry of humanity is for peace, peace."

Clearly a combination of factors, including the Papal pleading, got to Khrushchov.

John Kennedy was working through many trusted channels. His brother, Attorney General Robert F. Kennedy, held a secret meeting with the Soviet Ambassador in Washington, Anatoly Dobrynin, conveying the idea of the U.S. withdrawing the nuclear weapons from Turkey, in exchange for the withdrawal of the Soviet missiles from Cuba.

On Oct. 26, 1962, *Pravda* published, in full, the Pope's letter to Khrushchov. Two days later, Kennedy and Khrushchov reached the agreement that ended the Cuban missile crisis. Among the pledges made by Kennedy that avoided thermonuclear war was the promise that the United States would never invade Cuba. Kennedy made that pledge public in the press conference he gave immediately following the agreement with Khrushchov.

Unpublicized but crucial to the resolution of the crisis, was Kennedy's agreement to remove medium-range ballistic missiles from Turkey.

## Prospects to End the Cold War?

On Dec. 11, 1962, Premier Khrushchov wrote a lengthy, substantive secret letter to President Kennedy. He began:

DEAR MR. PRESIDENT, It would seem that

you and we have come now to a final stage in the elimination of tensions around Cuba. Our relations are already entering now their normal course since all those means placed by us on the Cuban territory which you considered offensive are withdrawn, and you ascertained that, to which effect a statement was already made by your side.

That is good. We appreciate that you just as we approached not dogmatically the solution of the question of eliminating the tension which evolved, and this enabled us under existing conditions to find also a more flexible form of verification of the withdrawal of the above mentioned means. Understanding and flexibility displayed by you in this matter are highly appreciated by us, though our criticism of American imperialism remains in force because that conflict was indeed created by the policy of the United States with regard to Cuba.

Khrushchov went on to confirm:

that we have removed our means from Cuba relying on your assurance that the United States and its allies will not invade Cuba....

Within a short period of time we and you have lived through a rather acute crisis. The acuteness of it was that we and you were already prepared to fight, and this would lead to a thermonuclear war. Yes, to a thermonuclear world war with all its dreadful consequences. We took it into account and, being convinced that mankind would never forgive the statesmen who would not exhaust all possibilities to prevent catastrophe, agreed to a compromise.

Khrushchov extended his wishes that President Kennedy would be re-elected and would serve another six years during which time U.S.-Soviet relations could advance considerably:

We believe that you will be able to receive a mandate at the next election too, and that you will be the U.S. President for six years, which would appeal to us. At our times, six years in world politics is a long period of time and during that period, we could create good conditions for peaceful coexistence on earth and this would be highly appreicated by the peoples of our countries as well as by all other peoples.

Khrushchov concluded with the proposal to continue and deepen the personal dialogue:

Now it is of special importance to provide for the possibility of an exchange of opinion through confidential channels which you and I have set up and which we use.... Let us, Mr. President, eliminate promptly the consequences of the Cuban crisis and get down to solving other questions, and we have them in number.

Khrushchov enumerated the question of the pending nuclear test ban treaty, the larger issue of disarmament and the unsettled issues of Germany and Berlin. He concluded:

Please, excuse me for my straightforwardness and frankness, but I believe as before that a frank and straightforward exchange of opinion is needed to avoid the worst. Please convey to your wife and your family wishes of good health from myself, my wife and my entire family.

In the wake of the Kennedy-Khrushchov exchange and the solving of the Cuban Missile Crisis, the White House and the Kremlin established a teletype "Hotline," and, on July 25, 1963, the two superpowers signed the first Limited Nuclear Test Ban Treaty.

In June 1963, in a commencement speech at American University, President Kennedy issued a call for an end to the Cold War altogether:

For, in the final analysis," he declared, "our most basic common link is that we all inhabit this small planet. We all breathe the same air. We all cherish our children's future. And we are all mortal.

# The Kennedy-Khrushchov Secret Correspondence

*All told, between the day after John F. Kennedy's election as President of the United States in Nov. 1960, through the days immediately preceding his assassination on Nov. 22, 1963, JFK and Soviet Premier Nikita Khrushchov exchanged more than 100 secret letters. In recent years, the entire correspondence has been declassified and made available through the U.S. Department of State Office of the Historian, in Volume VI of* Foreign Relations of the United States, 1961-1963.

While it is worthwhile to read the entire correspondence, to get a real insight into the statecraft that set the basis for averting thermonuclear war during the Cuban Missile Crisis of Oct. 1962, the following sampling of President Kennedy's letters to Khrushchov provide an invaluable insight into the awesome responsibilities that Kennedy and Khrushchov shared as the two world leaders who had it in their power to bring an end to humankind.

There is a profound lack of such statesmanship today. We have seen this, most clearly, in the actions of successive Bush and Obama administrations, which squandered away the opportunities posed by the end of the Cold War, and now, once again have brought the world to a near-term threat of thermonuclear extinction.

Use this sampling of the Kennedy-Khrushchov letters as a mirror through which to judge the current crisis of mankind—and the way out.

## 7. Letter From President Kennedy to Chairman Khrushchov

Washington, February 22, 1961.
DEAR MR. CHAIRMAN:
I have had an opportunity, due to the return of Ambassador Thompson, to have an extensive review of all aspects of our relations with the Secretary of State and with him. In these consultations, we have been able to explore, in general, not only those subjects which are of

U.S. National Archives

*August 1961: The Soviet-allied German Democratic Republic (East Germany) began building the Berlin Wall, dividing East Berlin from West Berlin.*

direct bilateral concern to the United States and the Soviet Union, but also the chief outstanding international problems which affect our relations.

I have not been able, in so brief a time, to reach definite conclusions as to our position on all of these matters. Many of them are affected by developments in the international scene and are of concern to many other governments. I would, however, like to set before you certain general considerations which I believe might be of help in introducing a greater element of clarity in the relations between our two countries. I say this because I am sure that you are conscious as I am of the heavy responsibility which rests upon our two Governments in world affairs. I agree with your thought that if we could find a measure of cooperation on some of these current issues this, in itself, would be a significant contribution to the problem of insuring a peaceful and orderly world.

I think we should recognize, in honesty to each other, that there are problems on which we may not be able to agree. However, I believe that while recognizing that we do not and, in all probability will not, share a common view on all of these problems, I do believe that the manner in which we approach them and, in particular, the manner in which our disagreements are handled, can be of great importance.

In addition, I believe we should make more use of diplomatic channels for quite informal discussion of these questions, not in the sense of negotiations (since I

am sure that we both recognize the interests of other countries are deeply involved in these issues), but rather as a mechanism of communication which should, insofar as is possible, help to eliminate misunderstanding and unnecessary divergencies, however great the basic differences may be.

I hope it will be possible, before too long, for us to meet personally for an informal exchange of views in regard to some of these matters. Of course, a meeting of this nature will depend upon the general international situation at the time, as well as on our mutual schedules of engagements.

I have asked Ambassador Thompson to discuss the question of our meeting. Ambassador Thompson, who enjoys my full confidence, is also in a position to inform you of my thinking on a number of the international issues which we have discussed. I shall welcome any expression of your views. I hope such exchange might assist us in working out a responsible approach to our differences with the view to their ultimate resolution for the benefit of peace and security throughout the world. You may be sure, Mr. Chairman, that I intend to do everything I can toward developing a more harmonious relationship between our two countries.

Sincerely,

John F. Kennedy

## 19. Telegram From President Kennedy to Chairmen Khrushchov and Brezhnev

Washington, July 4, 1961.

I wish to thank you personally and on behalf of the American people for your greetings on the occasion of the 185th Anniversary of the Independence of the United States. It is a source of satisfaction to me that on our 185th Anniversary the United States is still committed to the revolutionary principles, of individual liberty and national freedom for all peoples, which motivated our first great leader. I am confident that given a sincere desire to achieve a peaceful settlement of the issues which still disturb the world's tranquillity we can, in our time, reach that peaceful goal which all peoples so ardently desire. A special responsibility at this time rests upon the Soviet Union and the United States. I wish to assure the people of your country of our desire to live in friendship and peace with them.

John F. Kennedy

## 22. Letter From President Kennedy to Chairman Khrushchov

Hyannis Port, October 16, 1961.

DEAR MR. CHAIRMAN:

I regret that the press of events has made it impossible for me to reply earlier to your very important letter of last month. I have brought your letter here with me to Cape Cod for a week-end in which I can devote all the time necessary to give it the answer it deserves.

My family has had a home here overlooking the Atlantic for many years. My father and brothers own homes near my own, and my children always have a large group of cousins for company. So this is an ideal place for me to spend my weekends during the summer and fall, to relax, to think, to devote my time to major tasks instead of constant appointments, telephone calls and details. Thus, I know how you must feel about the spot on the Black Sea from which your letter was written, for I value my own opportunities to get a clearer and quieter perspective away from the din of Washington.

I am gratified by your letter and your decision to suggest this additional means of communication. Certainly you are correct in emphasizing that this correspondence must be kept wholly private, not to be hinted at in public statements, much less disclosed to the press. For my part the contents and even the existence of our letters will be known only to the Secretary of State and a few others of my closest associates in the government. I think it is very important that these letters provide us with an opportunity for a personal, informal but meaningful exchange of views. There are sufficient channels now existing between our two governments for the more formal and official communications and public statements of position. These letters should supplement those channels, and give us each a chance to address the other in frank, realistic and fundamental terms. Neither of us is going to convert the other to a new social, economic or political point of view. Neither of us will be induced by a letter to desert or subvert his own cause. So these letters can be free from the polemics of the cold war debate. That debate will, of course, proceed, but you and I can write messages which will

U.S. Army

*Fall 1961: Soldiers from the U.S. Army Berlin Command face off against police from East Germany.*

be directed only to each other.

The importance of this additional attempt to explore each other's view is well-stated in your letter; and I believe it is identical to the motivation for our meeting in Vienna. Whether we wish it or not, and for better or worse, we are the leaders of the world's two greatest rival powers, each with the ability to inflict great destruction on the other and to do great damage to the rest of the world in the process. We therefore have a special responsibility—greater than that held by any of our predecessors in the pre-nuclear age—to exercise our power with the fullest possible understanding of the other's vital interests and commitments. As you say in your letter, the solutions to the worlds most dangerous problems are not easily found—but you and I are unable to shift to anyone else the burden of finding them. You and I are not personally responsible for the events at the conclusion in World War II which led to the present situation in Berlin. But we will be held responsible if we cannot deal peacefully with problems related to this situation.

The basic conflict in our interests and approach will probably never disappear entirely, certainly not in our lifetime. But, as your letter so wisely points out, if you and I cannot restrain that conflict from leading to a vicious circle of bitter measures and countermeasures, then the war which neither of us or our citizens want—and I believe you when you say you are against war—

will become a grim reality.

I like very much your analogy of Noah's Ark, with both the clean and the unclean determined that it stay afloat. Whatever our differences, our collaboration to keep the peace is as urgent—if not more urgent—than our collaboration to win the last world war. The possibilities of another war destroying everything your system and our system have built up over the years—if not the very systems themselves—are too great to permit our ideological differences to blind us to the deepening dangers of such a struggle.

I, too, have often thought of our meeting in Vienna and the subsequent events which worsened the relations between our two countries and heightened the possibilities of war. I have already indicated that I think it unfruitful to fill this private channel with the usual charges and counter-charges; but I would hope that, upon re-examination, you will find my television address of July 25th was more balanced than belligerent, as it is termed by your letter, although there may have been statements of opinion with which you would naturally disagree. To be sure, I made it clear that we intended to defend our vital interests in Berlin, and I announced certain measures necessary to such a defense. On the other hand, my speech also made it clear that we would prefer and encourage a peaceful solution, one which settled these problems, in the words of your letter, on a mutually acceptable basis. My attitude concerning Berlin and Germany now, as it was then, is one of reason, not belligerence. There is peace in that area now—and this government shall not initiate and shall oppose any action which upsets that peace.

You are right in stating that we should all realistically face the facts in the Berlin and German situations—and this naturally includes facts which are inconvenient for both sides to face as well as those which we like. And one of those facts is the peace which exists in Germany now. It is not the remains of World War II but the threat of World War III that preoccupies us all. Of course, it is not normal for a nation to be divided by two different armies of occupation this long after the war; but the fact is that the area has been peaceful—it is not in itself the source of the present tension—and it could not be rendered more peaceful by your signing a peace treaty with the East Germans alone.

On the contrary, there is very grave danger that it might be rendered less peaceful, if such a treaty should convince the German people that their long-cherished hopes for unification were frustrated, and a spirit of na-tionalism and tension should sweep over all parts of the country. From my knowledge of West Germany today, I can assure you that this danger is far more realistic than the alleged existence there of any substantial number of Hitlerites or revanchists. The real danger would arise from the kind of resentment I have described above; and I do not think that either of us, mindful of the lessons of history, is anxious to see this happen. Indeed, your letter makes clear that you are not interested in taking any step which would only be exacerbating the situation. And I think this is a commendable basis on which both of us should proceed in the future.

The area would also be rendered less peaceful if the maintenance of the West's vital interests were to become dependent on the whims of the East German regime. Some of Mr. Ulbricht's statements on this subject have not been consistent with your reassurances or even his own—and I do not believe that either of us wants a constant state of doubt, tension and emergency in this area, which would require an even larger military build-up on both sides.

So, in this frank and informal exchange, let us talk about the peace which flows from actual conditions of peace, not merely treaties that bear that label. I am certain that we can create such conditions—that we can, as you indicate, reach an agreement which does not impair the vital interests or prestige of either side—and that we can transform the present crisis from a threat of world war into a turning-point in our relations in Europe.

What is the framework for such an agreement? Detailed proposals must be a matter of allied agreement on our side; and formal discussion must wait further exploration of specific items. Your letter indicates, however, that you are concerned over how protracted formal diplomatic negotiations can become, with each side asking for the utmost at the outset, making more statements to the press and using extreme caution in feeling out the other side.

I agree with you that these letters should be able to supplement and thus facilitate such negotiations. We are both practical men and these are meant to be private, frank exchanges. I can tell you, for example, that I recognize how difficult it would be to secure your agreement on a plan to reunify Germany by self-determination in the near future (as desirable as I think that is), just as you recognize that we could not be a party to any agreement which legalized permanently the present abnormal division of Germany. That is one reason why we could not be a party to a peace treaty with the East

Germans alone, even though, as I said at the UN, we do not view as a critical issue the mere signing by you of such a document. What is crucial, however, is the result which you have asserted that such a signing would have with respect to our basic rights and obligations.

I agree with the statement in your letter that our two governments must, in one framework or another, continue our obligations to assist in the unification into one entity of both German states if the Germans so desire. While, as you point out, the method of achieving this goal is properly a subject for discussion among the Germans themselves, this does not excuse us from the responsibility we have assumed since the war to see the country peacefully unified—and this is the reason why we cannot attempt any final legalization as a formal international frontier of the present line of demarcation between the Western and Eastern zones. It also enjoins us against any action which would retard movement across this line—although, not being blind, as you say, we cannot fail to recognize that this line does exist today as the Western limit of East German authority.

Whatever action you may take with East Germany, there is no difficulty, it seems to me, in your reserving your obligations and our rights with respect to Berlin until all of Germany is unified. But if you feel you must look anew at that situation, the real key to deciding the future status of West Berlin lies in your statement that the population of West Berlin must be able to live under the social and political system of its own choosing. On this basis I must say that I do not see the need for a change in the situation of West Berlin, for today its people are free to choose their own way of life and their own guarantees of that freedom. If they are to continue to be free, if they are to be free to choose their own future as your letter indicates in the phrase quoted above, I take it this includes the freedom to choose which nations they wish to station forces there (limited in number but with unrestricted access) as well as the nature of their own ties with others (including, within appropriate limits, whatever ties they choose with West Germany). Inasmuch as you state very emphatically that you have no designs on West Berlin—and I am glad to have this assurance, for it makes the prospects of negotiation much brighterI am sure you are not insisting on the location of Soviet troops in that portion of the city.

Thus, although there is much in your letter that makes me doubtful about the prospects in Germany, there are many passages which lead me to believe that an accommodation of our interests is possible. But in our view the situation should be peaceful now, and existing rights and obligations are already clear. What is not clear is how any change would be an improvement. Your letter and earlier aide-memoire, and Mr. Gromyko in his conversations with Mr. Rusk and myself, have made clear what you would hope to gain by a change—a new status for the East German regime, a settlement of frontiers, and relief from what you regard as potential dangers in West Germany—but it is not clear how we in the West are to benefit by agreeing to such a change. It is not enough to say there will be a free city in a city that is already free—or that there will be guarantees of our access when the old guarantees are still binding—or that we can maintain token troops in a city when we have troops there now.

You are, as I said before, a practical man; and you can see that there is no way in which negotiations on that basis could conceivably be justified on our part. We would be buying the same horse twice—conceding objectives which you seek, merely to retain what we already possess. I hope you will give long and serious thought to this question—for the kind of mutually acceptable settlement you mention is possible only if it brings actual improvements, from the standpoints of both parties.

The alternative is so dire that we cannot give up our efforts to find such a settlement. In the weeks ahead, while we are consulting on these matters with our respective allies and you are meeting with your Party Congress, I hope these efforts can continue—both through this correspondence and through other contacts. Let us also both strive during this period to avoid any statement, incident, or other provocation in Berlin which make a proper negotiating climate impossible. For the present, I believe we can agree on Ambassador Thompson as a very acceptable means of continuing the conversation. He knows of this letter; he has my complete confidence, and I am glad that this channel is satisfactory to you. He is in Washington at present, and will return to Moscow after our inter-Allied talks are further under way.

As for another meeting between the two of us, I agree completely with your view that we had better postpone a decision on that until a preliminary understanding can be reached through quieter channels on positive decisions which might appropriately be formalized at such a meeting. This reminds me that your letter also very graciously stated your desire to have me visit your country. If we can reach a reasonable settlement of Berlin and if the international atmosphere im-

Abbie Rowe/White House. John F. Kennedy Presidential Library and Museum, Boston

*President Kennedy meeting with his Ambassador to Moscow, Llewellyn Thompson, in 1961.*

proves, I would take great pleasure in such a visit. I visited the Soviet Union in 1932 very briefly, and would look forward to seeing the great changes that have occurred since then.

Let me make it clear that I do not intend to relegate the achievement of complete and general disarmament to a place of secondary importance. I share your conviction that nothing would do more to promote good will among nations and contribute to the peaceful solution of other major disputes. Our agreement on the statement of principles jointly submitted to the UN General Assembly, while barely a beginning on a matter where we remain far apart, at least holds out the hope that we may someday achieve the final stage of such disarmament, verified to remove the fears of any people that devastation may ever again be suddenly rained upon them.

At the same time, however, our attention is urgently needed on those current problems which keep the world poised on the brink of war. The situation in Laos is one example. Indeed I do not see how we can expect to reach a settlement on so bitter and complex an issue as Berlin, where both of us have vital interests at stake, if we cannot come to a final agreement on Laos, which we have previously agreed should be neutral and independent after the fashion of Burma and Cambodia. I do not say that the situation in Laos and the neighboring area must be settled before negotiations begin over Germany and Berlin; but certainly it would greatly improve the atmosphere.

It is now clear that Prince Souvanna Phouma will become the new Prime Minister if an agreement can be reached. But the composition of his government is far from settled, and without assuming either the knowledge or the power to select individual men for individual posts, you and I do have an obligation—if we are to reach our goal—to continue, in your words, using our influence on the corresponding quarters in Laos to make certain that Souvanna Phouma is assisted by the kind of men we believe necessary to meet the standard of neutrality. That standard is not met if the eight posts assigned to Souvanna are filled in a manner which heavily weights the scales in favor of one side or the other.

As you note, the withdrawal of foreign troops from the territory of Laos is an essential condition to preserving that nation's independence and neutrality. There are other, similar conditions, and we must be certain that the ICC has the power and the flexibility to verify the existence of these conditions to the satisfaction of everyone concerned.

In addition to so instructing your spokesmen at Geneva, I hope you will increasingly exercise your influence in this direction on all of your corresponding quarters in this area; for the acceleration of attacks on South Viet-Nam, many of them from within Laotian territory, are a very grave threat to peace in that area and to the entire kind of world-wide accommodation you and I recognize to be necessary. If a new round of measures and counter-measures, force and counter-force, occurs in that corner of the globe, there is no foretelling how widely it may spread. So I must close, as I opened, by expressing my concern over where current events are taking us.

My wife who is here with me reciprocates your good wishes, and we return the wish of good health to you and all your family. As I recall, I shall be seeing your son-in-law again in the not too distant future, and I look forward to talking with him.

I hope you will believe me, Mr. Chairman, when I say that it is my deepest hope that, through this exchange of letters and otherwise, we may improve relations between our nations, and make concrete progress in deeds as well as words toward the realization of a just and enduring peace. That is our greatest joint responsibility—and our greatest opportunity.

Sincerely,
John F. Kennedy